Christ and the Disciples

The miracle of the loaves and the fishes

CHRIST AND THE DISCIPLES

The Destiny of an Inner Community

PETER SELG

2011
STEINERBOOKS

A great deal of mystery is associated with the Christ's transformation into an earthly human being.

— RUDOLF STEINER[1]

SteinerBooks
610 Main Street, Great Barrington, MA 01230
www.steinerbooks.org

Copyright 2011 Peter Selg. All rights reserved. No part of this publication may be reproduced, stored in a retrieval system, or transmitted, in any form or by any means, electronic, mechanical, photocopying, recording, or otherwise, without the prior written permission of the publisher.

Translated by Catherine E. Creeger.

The illustrations in the text are by the Master of the Registrum Gregorii and other anonymous artists from the Codex Egberti, a tenth-century Ottonian manuscript, Stadbibliothek Trier, Germany.

Originally published in German as *Christus und die Jünger: Vom Schicksal der inneren Gemeinschaft* by Verlag des Ita Wegman Instituts 2009.

Library of Congress Cataloging-in-Publication Data

Selg, Peter, 1963-
 [Christus und die Jünger. English]
 Christ and the disciples : the destiny of an inner community /Peter Selg ; [translated by Catherine E. Creeger].
   p. cm.
 Includes bibliographical references
 ISBN 978-0-88010-745-7
 1. Jesus Christ – Anthroposophical interpretations.
 2. Apostles. 3. Anthroposophy – Doctrines. I. Title.
 BP596.J4S4513 2011
 299'.935 – dc23
                                      2011030696

Contents

Preface	1
1. Finding the Disciples	5
2. Christ's Activity in the Circle of Disciples	19
3. Gethsemane and Golgotha	53
4. The Disciples of the Risen One	85
5. Ascension and Pentecost	105
Appendix	129
Notes	135
About the Ita Wegman Institute	149

Preface

> There was something miraculous
> about this group of people.
> — Rudolf Steiner[2]

Hidden events that took place between the Christ and the community of his disciples form a significant part not only of the four Gospels, but also of the Christ mystery, or Golgotha mystery, itself. Still today, many souls are moved by this apostolic community: by how the disciples accompanied Christ Jesus, by their place in history (as an esoteric circle charged with an exoteric task), by their failures, and by the great new dawn that showed them the way after Pentecost. The disciples' situation was unique: According to the testimony of the Luke Gospel, the Christ said to them, "Happy the eyes that see what you are seeing!" (Luke 10:23).[3] For three years, the disciples were close to Christ, shared his life, and received a great deal of instruction from him, often in their own intimate circle away from public view. They were there when Christ performed healings and even when he prayed: "One day when he was praying alone in the presence of his disciples..." (Luke 9:18).

"For those around him, the life of Christ Jesus was a religious rite taking place in reality. The great sacrifice of the Mass was enacted on Golgotha," said Rudolf Steiner in a lecture to theologians.[4] Yet with the exception of John, all of the disciples fled from Golgotha, abandoning Christ Jesus to a lonely death on the cross. Friedrich Rittelmeyer once described this group as "a few pitiful disciples"—pitiful also with regard to their belated spiritual awakening.[5]

Rudolf Steiner once said that we in the twentieth and twenty-first centuries must live with the "etheric Christ" in the earth's aura in the same way that "the disciples once lived with Christ Jesus on the physical plane."[6] If this is so, it is essential for us to focus on the community of Christ's disciples. Rudolf Steiner himself made major contributions to illuminating the depths of the disciples' relationship and life with the Christ, both during the three years of his earthly life and after the Resurrection. An essential element of Steiner's life work was to apply "anthroposophically oriented cognition" to events of the beginning of the Christian era in order to "bring the Gospels' deeper content to the light of day."[7] Rudolf Steiner spoke in detail about the Christ's community of disciples in many lecture cycles; and in his lectures on the Fifth Gospel (given in 1913-1914), he shed light on this community from the perspective of the processes of human consciousness that were intimately involved in events at the beginning of the new era and that were inscribed in the chronicle of evolution, the akashic record.[8] As Sergei Prokofieff said, "Rudolf Steiner's communications from the realm of the Fifth Gospel are both the center and the culmination of anthroposophical Christology."[9]

In his lectures on the Fifth Gospel, and elsewhere, Rudolf Steiner opened up many perspectives that help us understand what took place between Christ and his disciples. This book's purpose is to make those perspectives available and accessible. Although all of Steiner's statements on this subject have been published, they are widely scattered among his lectures, and remain unknown to many individuals who are deeply committed to the community of Christ's disciples and to anthroposophical Christology. In view of the challenges to consciousness we face in modern times (and also in dealing with Christianity and the Christ Event itself), it seems urgently important to present details of the positive and often illuminating results of Rudolf Steiner's research. As the Gospels put it, "Nobody lights a lamp and then covers it with a basin or puts it under the bed. On the contrary, he puts it on a lamp-stand so that those who come in may see the light. For there is nothing hidden that will not become public, nothing under cover that will not be made known and brought into the open" (Luke 8:16-17).

My own writing on Rudolf Steiner's work owes a debt of gratitude not only to studies by the priests Rudolf Frieling, Emil Bock, and Friedrich Rittelmeyer, who drew on the substance of anthroposophical spiritual science to significantly advance our understanding of the Gospels, but also to Sergei O. Prokofieff's profound contributions to anthroposophical Christology.

PETER SELG

Director of the Ita Wegman Institute for
Basic Research into Anthroposophy

Arlesheim, Switzerland
Epiphany 2009

The Baptism in the Jordan

1.
Finding the Disciples

There are infinite depths in the Gospel accounts … of how the Christ's disciples came to him and followed him.

— Rudolf Steiner[10]

"JESUS WAS WALKING BY THE SEA OF GALILEE when he saw two brothers, Simon, called Peter, and his brother Andrew, casting a net into the lake; for they were fishermen. Jesus said to them, 'Come with me, and I will make you fishers of men.' And at once they left their nets and followed him. He went on and saw another pair of brothers, James son of Zebedee and his brother John; they were in the boat with their father Zebedee, overhauling their nets. He called them, and at once they left the boat and their father, and followed him" (Matthew 4:18-22). According to Matthew and Mark, this is how Christ Jesus approached these four fishermen on the northwest shore of the lake in Galilee and summoned them to follow him: he "saw" his future disciples and "called" them to him.

According to John the Evangelist, however, Christ's initial encounter with individual disciples took place earlier, in Judea, on the day after the Baptism in the Jordan, and was indirectly initiated by John the Baptist:

> The next day John was standing with two of his disciples when Jesus passed by. John looked toward him and said, "There is the Lamb of God." The two disciples heard him say this, and followed Jesus. When he turned and saw them following him, he asked, "What are you looking for?" They said, "Rabbi" (which means "teacher"), "where are you staying?" "Come and see," he replied. So they went and saw where he was staying, and spent the rest of the day with him. It was then about four in the afternoon.
>
> One of the two who followed Jesus after hearing what John said was Andrew, Simon Peter's brother. The first thing he did was to find his brother Simon. He said to him, "We have found the Messiah" (which is Hebrew for

"Christ"). He brought Simon to Jesus, who looked at him and said, "You are Simon son of John. At your calling, your name will be Cephas" (that is, Peter, the Rock). (John 1:35-42)

According to this account, Simon Peter's brother and another of the Baptist's disciples actively approached Jesus, as Simon Peter also did, at his brother's suggestion, a short time later. Christ announced to Peter that he would be calling him to join him (note the future tense: "your name *will be* Cephas"). The next day, according to John the Evangelist, Jesus left for Galilee. At the beginning of this journey, he "found" another disciple. "The next day, Jesus decided to leave for Galilee. He met Philip... and said to him, 'Follow me'" (John 1:43-44). Later Christ also found Matthew, the customs officer, "and said to him, 'Follow me,' and Matthew rose and followed him" (Matthew 1:9-10).

Christ's first encounter with Simon Peter (and the other future disciples) took place directly after the Baptism and in the immediate vicinity of John the Baptist, who prepared the way for Christ's future activity. The Gospel writers do not reveal that the Christ spent a long time alone in the wilderness after this meeting, nor do they describe the occasion when the disciples met and were "called" by Christ in Galilee as a *second* encounter.[11] Nonetheless, when Christ Jesus first met Andrew and Simon Peter, Philip and Nathaniel, his struggle with the spiritual adversarial forces was still to come; his meeting with the disciples and followers of John the Baptist *preceded* the Temptation. In a sense, John's disciples anticipated the Christ Event, the incarnation of a divine being, when they found their way to Christ Jesus immediately after the Baptism. Rudolf Steiner tells us that John the Baptist had cultivated a community of individuals "capable of understanding the impending Christ Event."[12] "John baptized with water in order to call forth in some individuals the strength to know that the kingdom of the heavens had drawn near, so they could better understand who

Christ Jesus was."[13] Thus prepared, and with John's help, these individuals were then able to "find" the Christ immediately after his baptism in the Jordan.[14]

*

Rudolf Steiner's lectures based on the Fifth Gospel do not describe Christ's first meeting with the Baptist's disciples, but only how various individuals found their way to Christ after the Baptism in the Jordan and Christ's forty days in the wilderness. Not all of these people ultimately joined the intimate circle of twelve disciples or apostles, but all were deeply moved by the being of Christ. The corresponding description by Rudolf Steiner begins with the Temptation, when Christ struggled with the adversarial forces alone in the desert after the Baptism. By refusing to turn the earthly, mineral element into bread, Christ resisted the third temptation, presented by Ahriman alone; but the question of human work, nourishment, and money persisted, a "remnant" to be resolved in the future.[15] Christ returned from the wilderness forty days after the Baptism in the Jordan; that is, after the Mystery of the divinity's incarnation into the well-prepared constitution of Jesus. Jesus' experiences since adolescence, Rudolf Steiner said, were prerequisites to the event of Baptism.[16] Steiner then continued, describing Christ Jesus' inner situation and his further journey:

> When Christ Jesus left the wilderness, he felt that the Christ Spirit had united with and transcended everything he had lived and learned since age twelve. He no longer felt connected to all the old, barren aspects of humankind's evolution. He had become indifferent even to the language spoken around him, and for a time he remained mute. He wandered around Nazareth and then ever farther out into the countryside. He visited many places where he had formerly spent time as Jesus of Nazareth,

and there something strange happened. In silence, as if having nothing in common with his surroundings, Christ Jesus wandered from one inn to the next, and wherever he stayed, he worked for and with the people there. What Ahriman had said about bread had left a deep impression on him. Wherever he went, he met people he had worked with before. They recognized him, and he realized that Ahriman had ready access to them because they were forced to turn stones or minerals (or rather, metal or money, which is the same thing) into bread. Having no reason to seek out those who lived according to the moral precepts of Hillel or others, he stayed with those the other Gospels call "tax collectors and sinners," because they were the ones who had to turn stones into bread. He associated primarily with such people.

But then a strange thing happened. Many of these people recognized him because he had spent time with them two or three times before, during the time leading up to his thirtieth year. At that time, they had recognized his wise, gentle, loving nature. Ultimately, the great pain and suffering he had experienced since age twelve was transformed into the miraculous power of love, which flowed out in every word he spoke, like some mysterious force pouring out over those around him. Wherever he went, in every house and inn, he was dearly loved, and this love remained behind when he left those places and moved on. In these houses, many people talked about that dear man, Jesus of Nazareth, who had passed through their towns. And then, as if through the influence of cosmic laws, this happened: When the families with whom Jesus of Nazareth had worked sat around talking after sundown, as they liked to do, it was as if he were still present among them! They talked about the dear man who had spent time with them as Jesus of Nazareth, and they had much to say about his love and kindness and the warm, pleasant sensations that filled their souls when he lived under their roof. And then the aftereffects of his love streamed into many of these houses. When a family sat for hours talking about this guest, the image of Jesus of Nazareth entered the room as a vision that was shared by all members of the family. He visited them in spirit, or perhaps they created his spiritual image.

You can well imagine how these families experienced that shared vision and what it meant to them when he reappeared after being baptized by John in the Jordan. They recognized his outer appearance, but his eyes shone more brightly than before. They saw the transfigured face of the one they had so loved to see; they saw the man who had sat with them in spirit. Just imagine how they experienced his return. How extraordinary it was for the families of sinners and tax collectors, for the sick, the burdened, and the possessed, whose karma plagued them with all the demonic beings of that time!

Now Jesus of Nazareth's transformed nature revealed what he had become through the indwelling of the Christ. It showed itself especially to people like this. Having once known only his love, goodness, and gentleness, they had then been able to have a vision of him; but now it was like some magical power emanating from him. Where they had once felt merely comforted by his presence, they now felt healed. So they went and fetched their neighbors, who were also oppressed and plagued by demonic powers, and brought them to Jesus Christ. This is how it happened that Christ Jesus, after defeating Lucifer and receiving only a sting from Ahriman, was then able to bring about what the Bible always describes as driving out demons and healing the sick. He had seen demons when he lay as if dead on the heathens' sacrificial altar, and many of these demons now fled from those to whom he appeared as Christ Jesus. Just as Lucifer and Ahriman had done, these demons

> recognized him as their opponent.... Now he knew that living for daily bread is what separated human beings from the heavens and drove them to egotism and into Ahriman's clutches.
> As he wandered the countryside preoccupied with these thoughts, those who most deeply sensed the transformation in Jesus of Nazareth became his disciples and followed him. As he left the inns, he was followed by one or the other person with the most profound experience of what I just described, and soon a group of such disciples formed around him. All of these people were filled with a fundamental mood of soul that was totally new in a certain sense....[17]

Rudolf Steiner's testimony on the Fifth Gospel tells us that even before the events at the Jordan, what emanated from Jesus of Nazareth (his empathy, his "love, goodness, and gentleness," his ongoing suprasensory presence) already had very strong effects on those around him. After the Baptism and the struggle with Lucifer and Ahriman, the effect radiating from him intensified to the point of healing, to the great benefit of the poor, hardworking people now freed from illness and from Ahriman's demonic servants. Rudolf Steiner recounted that many people who had known Jesus of Nazareth from his earlier travels now experienced his "transformation," the enhancement of his being that resulted from the indwelling of Christ. According to the Fifth Gospel, those who became Christ's disciples "sensed the transformation in Jesus of Nazareth most profoundly." *"As he left the inns, he was accompanied by one or the other person who followed him...."* All this happened around the Sea of Galilee, where his meeting (or second meeting) with the "fishermen" also took place, and where he "called" them to follow him.

*

Rudolf Steiner also spoke in other contexts about the "simple" people who became Jesus' disciples.[18] He did not, however, go into further detail about "the unique way in which Christ Jesus found his disciples."[19] The disciples were individuals closely connected to Christ Jesus on the basis of their particular mode of experience and "unique karma."[20] They approached him, but they were also chosen or called by him. *"You did not choose me: I chose you"* (John 15:16). In the narrower sense, these words apply to the twelve apostles whom Christ Jesus had selected from among a larger number of disciples, at a certain point in time, providing them with specific tasks and powers. "He then went up into the hill-country and called the men he wanted..." (Mark 3:13). Even finding the first apostles (not all of whom were accepted into the circle of twelve), was no arbitrary process but a matter of cosmically directed destiny:

> After the Baptism by John, cosmic, spiritual forces totally uninfluenced by the laws of earthly evolution remained active in Christ Jesus.
>
> For the last three years of his life (from age thirty to thirty-three), as Jesus of Nazareth walked the earth as Christ Jesus in Palestine, the entire cosmic Christ Being was constantly working into him. The Christ was always subject to the influence of the entire cosmos; he did not take a single step without being influenced by cosmic forces. What took place here with Jesus of Nazareth was the continued fulfillment of his horoscope; what was happening to him at any given moment otherwise happens to a human being only at birth. How was this possible? The entire body of the Nathan Jesus remained receptive to the totality of forces from the cosmic spiritual hierarchies guiding our earth. If the entire spirit of the cosmos was working into Christ Jesus, who was it, then, who set out on the road to Capernaum or some other place? To be sure, this being walking the earth looked like any other

human being, but the forces that were active in him and directed his body were cosmic forces originating in the sun and stars. What Christ Jesus did depended on the totality of the cosmos in which the earth is embedded. That is why the Gospels so often hint at constellations in connection with Christ Jesus' actions. When we read in the John Gospel that Christ found his first disciples "about four in the afternoon," the spirit of the entire cosmos, in accordance with the circumstances of that particular time, was expressed in this reality.[21]

*

As Christ said in his farewell discourses immediately preceding the events on Golgotha, not only the "spirit of truth" emanating from the Father, but also the disciples would bear witness on his behalf. "And you also are my witnesses, *because you have been with me from the first*" (John 15:27). The Christ's first meeting with the disciples occurred at the beginning of the three years of his earthly activity, shortly after the mighty transformation of his being through the Baptism in the Jordan.[22] Cosmically connected to Christ Jesus, the disciples were a necessity for him, an indispensable element and a prerequisite not only to his earthly journey but also to subsequent events that would permanently unite the Christ Being with the earth. In his lectures, Rudolf Steiner said:

> It is expressed most beautifully in the John Gospel: *I could not exist without you....* The disciples are a necessity to Jesus; they are fertile ground for him to grow upon. This is a great and significant truth.[23]

> Christ Jesus knelt before his disciples because without them, he could not have become what he was. Christ Jesus needs the disciples in the same way that plants need

minerals and animals need plants. Although lord and master, he becomes the servant of all.[24]

The earth, as Rudolf Steiner has said, is Christ Jesus' actual "body" and the disciples the "seeds of grain" through which he worked into humanity.[25] At the same time, the closer circle of the apostles was intimately related to the being of Christ Jesus: they were an organ not only of his activity but of his very existence. They belonged to him as a twelvefold expression of Christ Jesus' existence on earth and of his actual body.[26] Furthermore, they were a reflection of the activity of his soul and spirit:

> A certain deep and intimate interaction existed between Christ's soul and the souls of the Twelve. All of the rich and varied processes in the Christ's soul, so significant for that time, were also reflected in the souls of the apostles, but divided into twelve parts so that each of the Twelve experienced a different partial "reflection" of what was going on in the Christ's soul. What happened in Christ Jesus' soul was like a great, harmonious symphony that was reflected in the soul of each of the Twelve like a part that can be played by one of twelve instruments.[27]

*

"If anyone comes to me without abandoning his father and mother, wife and children, brothers and sisters, even his own soul, he cannot be a disciple of mine. No one who does not carry his cross and come with me can be a disciple of mine" (Luke 14:26-27). As the central prerequisite to admission to the disciples' circle—above and beyond unique individual karma—Christ Jesus repeatedly emphasizes the willingness to begin anew, to overcome old bonds and obstacles, whether social or inner and personal. Christianity, said Rudolf Steiner, has created "spiritualized love...the yeast that transforms individuals from within, the sourdough leaven that makes the world rise. Christ has come to say, if you do not abandon your mother, your wife, and all physical bonds, you cannot be my disciple. This does not mean abolishing all natural connections. It means extending love beyond the family to all human beings, transforming love into a living, creative, transformative force."[28] With the advent of Christianity, this living, creative, transforming force is no longer bound to blood relationships but becomes "universal love for humankind, love that moves from soul to soul, from person to person."[29] Called by Christ Jesus, the sons of Zebedee had to leave their boat and their father. "All love based on natural connections must come to an end; individual must relate to individual, and soul to soul."[30] The Christ is the "representative of humanity," and the community that grows up around him serves a future humanity that will overcome the past. "All of these people were filled with a fundamental mood of soul that was totally new in a certain respect."

> We must interpret this not as rejection of justified relationships and filial love but as acknowledgment that Christ Jesus brings the divine spiritual principle into the world and that all human individuals, by virtue of being human, can discover this principle within, in the essential core of their being. Increasingly, people will be touched by the inmost mystery of Christianity, which leads beyond all differences among individuals to the universally human, to what every human being can discover within.[31]

In the circle of Christ Jesus' disciples, Rudolf Steiner said, an archetypal community or bond of brotherhood developed:

> In the human fraternity that must encompass the entire human race, we will all know this: because you are human, you are my brother. This is Christianity's most profound principle. The narrow-minded bonds of other relationships

must be shattered, and a common bond must link individual to individual. This shift, however, also shatters the ancient principle of initiation, which was based on blood relationships.[32]

The community of disciples became the bearer of "spiritual love."[33] This circle housed the *"foundation stone of a new world"* (Rittelmeyer[34]), a universal impulse of love as defined by the active spirit of Christ, his agape. "The spirit that increasingly floods the earth with this universal love is the Christ Spirit."[35] In his farewell discourses to the disciples, Christ says:

> I give you a new commandment: love one another; as I have loved you, so you are to love one another. If there is this love among you, then all will know that you are my disciples. (John 13:34-35)

> This is my commandment to you: love one another. (John 15:17)

Christ walking on the water

2.

Christ's Activity in the Circle of Disciples

More than simply participating in the healings performed by Christ Jesus himself, his closest friends and disciples were gradually imbued with the mighty power at work in Christ Jesus as it passed from him to them.

— Rudolf Steiner[36]

JESUS WAS THE DISCIPLES' spiritual teacher. Sometimes he spoke to them in mighty discourses (such as the Sermon on the Mount) intended for them alone; sometimes in confidential conversations when they were alone together; and sometimes in instructive explanations directed at them in the midst of large crowds. "In the hearing of all the people Jesus said to his disciples..." (Luke 20:45). At their request, he explained the parables he used in public speeches in greater detail. Mark writes, "He never spoke to them [the people] except in parables; but privately to his disciples he explained everything" (Mark 4:34). According to Luke, Christ said to the disciples, "It has been granted to you to know the secrets of the kingdom of God; but the others have only parables...." (Luke 8:10; the corresponding passages in Mark and Matthew are very similar.)

The disciples lived surrounded by Christ's teachings and internalized them, although certainly without understanding them completely. Rudolf Steiner described this process in various ways: The "enlivening, instructive power" of Christ Jesus passed over to them.[37] The disciples took in the "living, instructive forces" of Christ Jesus.[38] This "living instruction" took effect to a certain extent, although the disciples were incompletely prepared to receive it: "The forces they had already developed did not allow them to understand...."[39] Christ's word, however, was life and power, and the disciples often heard it in all its intensity and intimacy in locations protected and hidden from the public. Christ repeatedly "withdrew privately" with his disciples (Luke 9:10). *At the disciples' request*, he also instructed them in meditation. As Luke notes, that is how the Our Father was first spoken and conveyed: *"Lord, teach us to pray..."* (Luke 11:1). Rudolf Frieling writes:

Luke has recorded the circumstances under which the Our Father was communicated. Jesus had once again retreated into solitary prayer.[40] (Luke's words are, "Once, in a certain place, Jesus was at prayer.") When he paused, an unnamed disciple, clearly profoundly impressed by Christ's prayer, utters the request that was then so wonderfully answered. This time, the disciples are not content to simply be in the company of a lone individual at prayer; they want to pray actively themselves, and the Christ conveys to them a preliminary form of the Our Father.[41]

*

Rudolf Steiner said that Christ worked in the circle of disciples and on their developing community less through the spoken word than through the profound experience and spiritual assistance of his immediate presence. "Hearing his word actually did not carry as much weight as we experience today when listening to teachings. Christ Jesus' teaching, although always experienced as beneficial, was not what was perceived as most important."[42] "Christ Jesus' disciples simply knew that being in his presence meant something different than being around someone else. They knew him to be the vehicle of a superearthly being. Quite naturally, therefore, their suprasensory consciousness was kindled when they were together with him."[43] But as Rudolf Steiner explained in greater detail in different contexts, "being in Christ's presence" did not always mean that he was physically present:

> This clearly suggests that Christ's activity was not simply limited to the single personality of Jesus of Nazareth, but also affected the disciples from outside, as when he came walking toward them, out-of-body, over the lake. He was able to be in one place in his physical body yet elsewhere, out of the body, in his activity or impulse, the emanation

of his spirit, which streamed into his disciples' souls. The Mark Gospel makes it especially clear that what Christ preaches and teaches in the out-of-body state is perceived by individuals and fills their souls. It pervades and surrounds their souls, although they do not understand it. Its presence is both earthly and superearthly, in the individuality of the Christ and in the crowd.

The Christ is always associated with an extensive and active aura. This aura existed because he was united in soul with the people he had chosen, and it persisted as long as he remained connected to them.[44]

In lectures in Kassel in June of 1909, where he described the intensification of the Christ's power over the course of the three years, Rudolf Steiner explained these circumstances in more detail, taking as his starting point a corresponding passage from the Gospel according to John:

> "*Darkness had already fallen, and Jesus had not yet joined them. By now a strong wind was blowing and the sea grew rough. When they had rowed about three or four miles they saw Jesus walking on the sea and approaching the boat. They were terrified...*" (John 6:16-19). Bible editors today tend to insert the highly superfluous title "Jesus walks on water," as if that phrase appeared anywhere in this chapter. Where does it say "Jesus walks on water"? Here it is: "The disciples saw Jesus walking on the sea." We must take the Gospels literally. Once again, the Christ's power has intensified. Through his recent actions, it was enhanced beyond the point where the Christ's soul simply communicated itself to other souls. He could now appear in his own form to other souls suited to perceiving it. What is happening here? He is somewhere else, but his power is so strong that it works on others far away. The Christ's power is now so strongly active that it does more

than simply trigger power in the disciples, as happened to those who were together on with him on the mountain. In that instance, his power passed over into the disciples and brought about the miracle [of the feeding of the multitude]. Now, however, they have the power to see the Christ in his own form, even though their physical eyes cannot see where he is. The Christ can now become visible from a distance to those already joined to him by bonds of soul. Now his own form has developed to the point of becoming spiritually visible. When physical vision becomes impossible for the disciples, spiritual vision becomes all the stronger and they behold the Christ. When seeing at a distance like this, however, the image of the object is the same as if it were close at hand.[45]

The disciples, Rudolf Steiner said, beheld the figure of the Christ and experienced his "immediate presence" as if he were actually there with them. In a later lecture, Steiner said that there on the lake, the disciples perceived the "nocturnal power of the sun" reflected by Christ, a cosmic power that flows toward them through the intermediary of the Christ. ("As Christ Jesus walked the earth in Palestine, his personality and individuality provided the medium through which the power of the sun worked into our earth. [The Gospels] always suggest the position of the sun in relationship to the constellations, the manna from heaven. These instances refer to this cosmic character, this influx of cosmic forces through the Christ."[46]) Mark describes the nocturnal scene on the Sea of Galilee in these words: "It grew late and the boat was already well out on the water, while he was alone on the land. Somewhere between three and six in the morning, seeing them laboring at the oars against a headwind, he came toward them, walking on the lake. He was going to pass them by; but when they saw him walking on the lake, they thought it was a ghost and cried out; for they all saw him and were terrified. But at once he spoke to them: 'Take heart! I am here; do not be afraid.' Then he climbed into the boat beside them, and the wind dropped. At this they were completely dumbfounded..." (Mark 6:47-52).

*

In his lectures on the Fifth Gospel in October 1913 in Kristiania (Oslo), Rudolf Steiner spoke for the first time in detail about the Christ's different ways of being present in the circle of disciples during his time on earth. Steiner had already hinted at certain individual aspects in earlier observations on the Gospels, but now he described the entire process of the three years (and specifically Christ's suprasensory presence in the circle of disciples) in greater detail against the background of Christ's ever-increasing incarnation. In Kristiania, Rudolf Steiner said that in the three years after the Baptism in the Jordan, Christ united ever more deeply with the physical nature of Jesus. ("At the beginning of his three-year earthly journey, the being of Christ was only loosely connected to the three bodies of Jesus, but it was drawn ever more deeply into those bodies as time when on."[47] Initially, there were repeated instances of the purely spiritual presence of Christ without the presence of the physical nature of Jesus. Rudolf Steiner said such instances must be taken into account in seeking a deeper understanding of Gospel accounts:

> The Fifth Gospel shows us that the body of Jesus of Nazareth was not always present when the Christ Being appeared to the apostles. Often that body remained somewhere else and only the Christ Spirit appeared to the apostles. In these instances, however, his appearance was such that they easily confused the spiritual phenomenon with the body of Jesus of Nazareth. They certainly noticed a difference, but it was so slight they did not always pay attention to it. This state of affairs is not so clearly addressed

in the four Gospels, but the Fifth Gospel makes it obvious that the apostles could not always clearly distinguish Christ in the body of Jesus of Nazareth from Christ as a purely spiritual being. The difference was not always apparent; in any given instance, they did not always know what they were seeing. They did not give the matter much thought, but they generally took this phenomenon to be Christ Jesus—that is, the Christ Spirit—inasmuch as they recognized him in the body of Jesus of Nazareth.[48]

In a later lecture on the Fifth Gospel, on December 10, 1913, in Munich, Rudolf Steiner said:

This was the situation initially, when the Christ Being was not closely bound to the bodies of Jesus, but only loosely and superficially. At times the Christ Being was outwardly united with the three bodies of Jesus of Nazareth and appeared in them among the disciples and his closest followers, speaking to them in this guise. That was not always necessary, however. While these outer sheaths were in some other place, the Christ Being was able to extricate himself from them and appear somewhere else, far away. In many instances, only the Christ Being appeared to the disciples, followers, and others.[49]

Early in the Christ's three years on earth between his baptism in the Jordan and death on the cross of Golgotha, the Christ Being "permeated" the physical nature of Jesus but did not fully imbue it as a truly incarnated "I." "This being took hold of these three bodies only weakly, like a mighty aura."[50] Rudolf Steiner said that during this time the spiritual being of the Christ disengaged from the physical body "countless times." Christ's spirit being (or spirit body) was so strong, however, "that he was always perceived as a physical presence. ...According to the Fifth Gospel, when the other Gospels speak of the disciples being together with the Christ, he was often present as a phenomenon that was not physical *but merely visionary, enhanced to the point of apparent physical presence.*"[51] Rudolf Steiner told that this state of affairs was characteristic of the first year of Christ's three earthly years. "In the first year, the Christ was only loosely connected to the body of Jesus of Nazareth. In instances of all sorts, that physical body was in one place while the Christ Being was somewhere else. Wherever the other Gospels tell of the Lord appearing to his disciples in a certain place, the physical body was actually somewhere else while Christ walked the land in spirit. *That was the situation initially.*"[52]

According to the testimony of the Fifth Gospel, Christ seldom actually spoke to his disciples or to the public in Judea and Galilee during the early part of his three earthly years, directly following the Baptism and the Temptation. In that first, preliminary stage of union with an earthly body, he was still working through "pure presence," through the "mighty aura" of his spirit being. Steiner characterized Christ's presence and activity during this time as follows: "The unique way in which the Christ Being was connected to the physical nature of Jesus of Nazareth produced effects that emanated from him to other people, effects that were otherwise nonexistent in the Earth phase of evolution. We call the reflections of these effects "miracles," but the word is either totally inappropriate or at best poorly understood today. These effects emanating from him were the result of how his constitutional members interacted."[53]

*

In a lecture on the "miracle" of the loaves and fishes, Rudolf Steiner said:

> *"Then Jesus took the loaves, gave thanks, and distributed them to the people as they sat there. He did the same with the fishes, and they had as much as they wanted."* (John 6:11)

What is Christ Jesus doing? To do what must be done, he avails himself of the souls of the disciples who were with him and who had gradually matured to his stature. They surround him now and take part in his activity, for he can now awaken a benevolent force in their souls. His power streams out into the disciples.... Earlier, he had let his power stream into the soul of the man who had been sick for thirty-eight years. Now, his power works into the souls of the disciples. The array of forces becomes stronger, expanding from one soul to the souls of others. In other words, the activity of Christ's soul is also already present in the disciples' souls.

When people wonder what happens as the result of such influence, they should simply stick to experience, and attempt to observe what happened when the great power present in the Christ, instead of working alone, expanded its activity by kindling power in the souls of others. Today such a vital faith is not available to many people—they may believe theoretically, but not with sufficient energy. If they did, however, they would be able to observe what happened. Spiritual science, for example, is well aware of what was going on.

Here, therefore, we see a step-by-step enhancement of the Christ Power.[54]

The Christ Power worked into and upon the disciples' souls. As they distributed the bread and fishes among the crowd, Rudolf Steiner said, the power emanating from the "mighty ether body of Christ Jesus" was at work in them.[55] "What was it that the people ate? Not barley loves, but the power of the Christ's body. They were nourished by the power that emanated from Christ as a result of his giving thanks to the spheres from which he descended."[56] The intimate association the disciples developed shortly after their first meeting with Christ Jesus enabled them to pass on the Christ Power, which originates in divine spheres.

"The activity of Christ's soul is also already present in the disciples' souls."

"Christ Jesus' disciples simply knew that being in his presence meant something different than being around someone else. They knew him to be the vehicle of a superearthly being, and they felt touched by this superearthly being...." Rudolf Steiner said that the disciples became aware quite early of Christ Jesus' divine nature, the "mighty aura" of his spirit being. "They felt touched" by either the physical or purely spiritual presence of this superearthly being. Steiner indicated repeatedly that the intimate circle of disciples was made up of individuals with "atavistic clairvoyant" abilities, which allowed them to perceive the uniqueness of this situation. These same clairvoyant forces predestined them to find their way to the Christ and to increasingly deepen their connection to him. ("This is also why Christ Jesus' contemporaries, even those who loved him, could understand the Apostles, Christ's inner circle, only to the extent that they realized these disciples were equipped with atavistic clairvoyance. Because of this clairvoyance, they were dimly aware of what was going on around them in a way that their actual human forces did not permit."[57]) The disciples retained "aspects of old forms of cognition" that worked on a "completely instinctive level, without coming to clear consciousness in their souls."[58]

Through their association with Christ Jesus, however, the disciples were meant to further their development, to transcend their old mode of existence (and thus, themselves) "through the forces of Christ Jesus radiating into them. ...Their life and their living wisdom had to grow. They had to grow in a great variety of ways."[59] The suprasensory consciousness kindled in them through their association with Christ Jesus had to be further developed and strengthened—a central focus of Christ's instruction. Rudolf Steiner said that the disciples were meant to augment their "atavistic" capabilities with new, imaginative powers of cognition. The Christ explained his teaching parables to the disciples in greater detail to help them develop imaginative cognition in the sense of truly being able to participate in his own cognitive power. Rudolf Steiner tells us that the power of Christ's own imaginative perception was gradually vested in the disciples as he allowed it to "radiate" into them.[60] In two lectures, Steiner said:

> For those around Christ Jesus, it was not simply a question of acquiring the ability to hear his majestic pronouncements (such as the Sermon on the Mount), and to participate in the healings he performed. More than that, the mighty power at work in Christ Jesus was actually vested in them over a period of time.[61]

> What emanated from Christ Jesus worked in two ways. Those outside of his intimate circle heard his words and understood them on a somewhat theoretical basis. Others, however, had been chosen by him because their particular karma allowed him to transmit his own power to them, and these individuals experienced his power directly. Its effect on them was to trigger imaginations in their souls, insights that pointed toward the next level in the higher worlds. The real meaning of Matthew 13:11 is, "Those outside hear only parables (that is, symbolic expressions of events in the spiritual world), but you perceive the meaning of the parables and the words that guide you into higher worlds." We must not interpret this verse in any trivial sense; it means that the disciples were being guided up into higher worlds.[62]

> And what did the disciples see? In all-embracing images, they saw humanity's evolution; they saw the future, when human beings would gradually draw closer to the impulse of the Christ.[63]

On the basis of their "unique karma," Christ Jesus was able to vest his power in the disciples, freeing imaginations in their souls, "insights pointing toward the next level in the higher worlds." Christ Jesus "guided" his closest disciples up into the higher worlds, into the coming kingdom of God for which John the Baptist had prepared them. At least some of the disciples had been part of John's circle; through the Baptism in the Jordan, he had made them aware that "the most important impulse of earth's evolution was descending into an earthly body." And then the Christ Spirit actually did "descend" into the body of Jesus of Nazareth, and through it, into the earthly world.

With the Christ's descent, a cosmic power entered earthly circumstances. Through their "unique karma," these disciples gathered in the immediate vicinity of this power, entering into and dwelling in its sphere of activity. Rudolf Steiner said that Christ wanted to guide his disciples up into higher worlds. He was able to "unite his being with the forces of the stars and bring these forces into the physical world. Or, in other words, his specially prepared physical and etheric bodies, his whole being, enabled him to attract the power of the sun, the moon, and the stars—in short, of the entire cosmos related to our earth. His actions transmitted the healing, strengthening, life-giving forces that otherwise stream into human beings when they are outside of their physical and etheric bodies during sleep."[64] In the same lecture, Rudolf Steiner said of the disciples:

> The forces working through Christ Jesus were forces that streamed out of the cosmos. Attracted by his body, they streamed through it and poured out over his disciples. Because of their receptivity, the disciples were then truly able to feel that the Christ Jesus who stood before them was a being who nourished them spiritually with the outpouring forces of the cosmos.[65]

On the conscious level, however, what did this mean for the disciples?

They existed in a state of dual consciousness. They were not yet the most highly developed individuals, but they were pulling themselves up to a higher level of development through their association with the Christ. They themselves were always in a state of dual consciousness comparable to human waking and sleeping. They alternated between sleeping and waking, and in both states the magical power of the Christ worked on them; by day, when he approached them; but also during sleep, when they were outside of their physical and etheric bodies. Normally, people are unconscious of flowing out into the world of the stars during sleep, and know nothing about it, but in the disciples' case the Christ Power was with them; they became aware of it and recognized that it provided them with nourishment from the realm of the stars.

The disciples' dual consciousness, however, is also significant from another perspective. In any individual, even a disciple of Jesus, we must acknowledge two elements: first, what that person is now; and second, the potential he or she carries for development in incarnations leading far into the future. For example, the potential for a completely different view of your surroundings in a future cultural epoch is already there in each one of you. If you were to become clairvoyantly aware of this element, it would reveal the immediate future in an initial clairvoyant impression, of sorts. What will happen in the immediate future is among the earliest of clairvoyant experiences, at least if those experiences are pure, legitimate, and truthful. That was certainly the case with the disciples. In their normal waking state, the power of Christ flowed into them in ways they recognized as belonging to waking consciousness. But how was it for them during sleep? The fact that they were disciples of Jesus and that the Christ Power had worked on them meant that they always became clairvoyant at certain times during sleep. During those times, instead of seeing what was going on at the moment, they saw what human beings would be doing in the future. As if diving into the sea of astral vision, they saw what would happen in the future.

For the disciples, therefore, two states of consciousness existed. They recognized one as their daily waking state. In it, the Christ nourished them spiritually with forces from the vast expanses of the cosmos. As the power of the sun, he brought those forces down to them, transmitting to them the forces the sun contributes through the seven constellations of the day. That was the origin of their daily nourishment. Then at night, the disciples realized, they perceived how the Christ Power sent heavenly food into their souls through the nighttime sun, the sun that is invisible as it passes through the remaining five constellations.

This is how the disciples, in their imaginative clairvoyance, sensed their union with the Christ's sun power, which sent them what was right for the people of their time; that is, of the fourth cultural epoch. And in their other state of consciousness, the Christ Power sent them the forces of the nocturnal sun through the five constellations of the night, which, however, referred to the next (that is, the fifth) cultural epoch. That is what the disciples experienced.[66]

In this connection, Rudolf Steiner also explained the loaves and fishes that fed the multitudes:

> According to ancient designations, any large number of people was described as "a thousand," and it could be made more specific by adding a number derived from the most important characteristic. For example, the people of the fourth cultural epoch were described as the "fourth thousand," and those who were already living in the manner of the fifth cultural epoch were called the "fifth thousand." Those are simply technical terms. This, then, is

what the disciples realized: in our state of day-consciousness, we perceive what the Christ Power sends down from the sun's forces through the seven day constellations. Then we receive the food intended for the fourth thousand, the people of the fourth cultural epoch. And in our nocturnal state of imaginative clairvoyance, through the five night constellations, we perceive what is intended for the near future, for the fifth thousand.

Thus the people of the fourth epoch, the fourth thousand, are fed by seven heavenly loaves (the seven day constellations); while the people of the fifth epoch, the fifth thousand, are nourished by the five heavenly loaves (the five night constellations). And in both cases, the sign of the fishes indicates the dividing line between day and night constellations.

We touch on a mystery here. The feeding of the multitudes points to an important mystery process; that is, Christ's supernatural communion with the disciples. Christ makes it clear to them that he is not talking about the "old sourdough" of the Pharisees. Rather, he supplies them with heavenly food brought down from the Sun forces of the cosmos, feeding them even though nothing is available except the seven day loaves (day constellations) in one instance and five night loaves (nocturnal constellations) in the other, which are always separated by the fishes. Matthew even refers to two fishes, to make it especially obvious. (Matthew 14:13-31 and 15:32-38)[67]

*

Rudolf Steiner tells us that the "unique type of living instruction" the inner circle of disciples received from the Christ was truly a "transmission of forces" that emanated from him and radiated into the disciples' souls. Christ's teachings and existence were cosmic in nature:

In his being, he focused or collected forces that were meant to flow from the macrocosmos into earthly conditions and the disciples' souls. This channeling was possible only through forces united in the being of Christ Jesus. The instructive and enlivening forces of the cosmos itself, which otherwise flow into human beings only during the unconsciousness of sleep, streamed from cosmic expanses through the being of Christ to the disciples.[68]

Rudolf Steiner said that the disciples were to be initiated into the mysteries of existence in order to be able to shape the future. "Expanding into the macrocosm," however, is an essential part of any true initiation. "During initiation, individual candidates consciously grow into the macrocosm and learn about it bit by bit. The Christ, however, stepped out of the macrocosm, as it were, always revealing the forces at work in it and conveying them to the disciples."[69]

On their difficult path of consciousness, the disciples received much support, not only from Christ Jesus, but also once again from John the Baptist, Christ's forerunner "in the spirit and power of Elijah" (Luke 1:17). After Herod caused John's violent earthly death, the Baptist's individuality "continued to work like an aura, and Christ Jesus entered the field of this aura."[70] Rudolf Steiner tells us that the Elijah soul of the Baptist then became the "group soul" of the community of the apostles, "living on in the circle of the Twelve."[71] After the Baptist crossed the threshold and lent his support to the community of disciples for whom he had paved the way, Christ Jesus placed greater "demands" on the disciples' cognitive capacities. "He expected higher understanding from them."[72] Rudolf Steiner, describing the second feeding of the multitudes and the connection between Christ and the disciples, said:

> Now the Christ expects his disciples to understand the meaning of the multiplication of the loaves in a very

particular way. He had never spoken such words to them before. By now, however, they ought to understand the destiny of John the Baptist after his beheading by Herod, and they ought to understand what it means when the five loaves fed the five thousand and the crumbs filled twelve baskets, and when the seven loaves fed four thousand and the crumbs filled seven baskets. So Christ says to them, "'Have you no inkling yet? Do you still not understand? Are your minds closed? You have eyes; can you not see? You have ears; can you not hear? When I broke the five loaves among five thousand, how many baskets of scraps did you pick up?' 'Twelve,' they said. 'And how many when I broke the seven loaves among four thousand?' They answered, 'Seven.' He said, 'Do you still not understand?'" (Mark 8:17-21).

Why does he reproach them so severely for not being able to understand these revelations? He knows that the spirit of Elijah is now free, *living in the disciples*. They must now gradually show themselves worthy to receive him into their souls so they may understand higher things than they were formerly capable of understanding. Now that the spirit of Elijah has approached the Twelve like a group soul and pervaded them with a common aura, they have become, at least potentially, capable of clairvoyance in a higher sense. What they could not achieve singly, the Twelve could perceive together, illumined by the spirit of Elijah-John. That is what Christ was attempting to teach them.[73]

After the spirit of Elijah-John had passed into the community of disciples, surrounding and pervading them like a "common aura," it became more possible for the Christ to guide them further in understanding spiritual secrets. As Rudolf Steiner described, the spirit of Elijah-John continued to support the necessary growth and transformation of the disciples until the resurrection of Lazarus.[74]

And in fact, the disciples did make significant progress, even outwardly. With cosmic forces (to their own astonishment), they performed baptisms, disseminated Christ's teachings, and cured people of serious illnesses and infirmities. "They returned jubilant. 'In your name, Lord,' they said, 'even the demons submit to us'" (Luke 10:17). When the disciples "returned" to the Christ after their journeys, they were returning to the shared inner domain, the "lonely place" where they could "rest quietly" with him, in the sphere of his immediate power and activity (Mark 6:32).

*

"When he came to the territory of Caesarea Philippi, Jesus asked his disciples, 'Who do men say the Son of Man is?' They answered, 'Some say John the Baptist, others Elijah, others Jeremiah, or one of the prophets.' 'And you,' he asked, 'who do you say I am?' Simon Peter answered, *You are the Messiah, the Son of the living God.*' Then Jesus said, 'Simon son of Jonah, you are favored indeed! You did not learn that from mortal man; it was revealed to you by my heavenly Father.'" (Matthew 16:13-17). Peter's recognition or acknowledgment of the Christ, which took place in northern Galilee near Mount Hermon, six months before the death on the cross of Golgotha, was not a result of Peter's natural capacities. At that moment, the answer could not have emerged from Peter's normal mental powers. Christ Jesus, as he looked at Peter, had to wonder, where can this answer have come from, since it points to a time in the distant future? And when he looked at what Peter's consciousness already contained as a result of intellect or initiation, Christ knew that the answer had not come from conscious knowledge. More profound forces spoke through Peter, forces that would only gradually become conscious in human beings. Divine-spiritual forces, perhaps the deepest of any that lie far below the surface of consciousness in human beings, were speaking through him.[75]

In Luke's account of the same incident, Christ's question arises out of a state of prayer or meditation. "One day when he was praying alone in the presence of disciples, he asked them, 'Who do people say I am?'…'And you,' he said, 'who do you say I am?'" (Lk 9:18-20). Only now, after more than two years of travelling with the disciples, did Christ Jesus turn to them and ask whether they recognized his essential being. "God's Messiah," replied Peter appropriately, in a seminal statement which, however, did not correspond to his own day-consciousness. At that point, Christ Jesus began to talk to the disciples about events to come in Jerusalem, about Golgotha and his impending death. "From that time, Jesus began to make it clear to his disciples that he had to go to Jerusalem, and there to suffer much from the elders, chief priests, and doctors of the law; to be put to death and to be raised again on the third day" (Matthew 16:21). Peter, clearly past the peak of his spiritual experience, "took him by the arm and began to rebuke him. 'Heaven forbid!' he said. 'No, Lord, this shall never happen to you.' Then Jesus turned and said to Peter, 'Away with you, Satan; you are a stumbling-block to me. You think as men think, not as God thinks'" (Matthew 16:22-23).

Rudolf Steiner said that the Christ, building on the subconscious power present in Peter after his preceding profession of belief, began to speak for the first time about the impending Mystery of Golgotha but met with no reception in Peter's understanding and response:

> Now, however, the moment is past when a more profound element in Peter was able to speak. Now he speaks out of his existing consciousness, and he cannot understand what the Christ means; he cannot believe that suffering and dying must occur. When Peter speaks out of his consciously developed inner forces, Christ rebukes him, saying, "What is speaking now is no god but what you have cultivated as a human being. It does not deserve to emerge here; it comes

from deceptive teachings, from Ahriman, from Satan!" This is the meaning of Christ's words, "Away with you, Satan; you are a stumbling-block to me. You think as men think, not as God thinks." Christ makes a point of calling him Satan, which he uses to mean Ahriman, whereas in the Bible *diabolos* indicates the Luciferic element. In fact, the expression Christ uses is an accurate description of the illusion to which Peter will still succumb.[76]

Immediately after the Baptism, Christ was tempted in the wilderness, warding off the attacks of the adversarial powers as they attempted to lure him away from his wisdom-filled path toward Golgotha, long preordained in the spiritual world. The end of this journey, the earthly death of a divine being, was the ultimate purpose of the entire Christ Incarnation.[77] Peter's words, "This shall never happen to you," as a refusal to accept the fate of Golgotha, were also an expression of "adversarial" intention. Christ rebuked Peter and then spoke to the disciples about the cross (his own and theirs) for the first time:

> If anyone wishes to be a follower of mine, he must leave his self behind; he must take up his cross and come with me. Whoever cares for his own safety is lost; but if a man will let himself be lost for my sake, he will find his true self. What will a man gain by winning the whole world, at the cost of his true self? Or what can he give that will buy that self back? For the Son of Man is to come in the glory of his Father with his angels, and then he will give each man the due reward for what he has done. I tell you this: there are some of those standing here who will not taste death before they have seen the Son of Man coming in his Kingdom. (Matthew 16:24-28)

"They did not understand that they, his companions, were destined to experience the powerful effect of that "I," of the

Christ Principle, and were meant to ascend into the spiritual world directly through it."[78] Within a week, however, Christ's Transfiguration on Mount Tabor would give them a provisional experience of beholding the coming of the Son of Man "in his kingdom" or "in the Kingdom of God."

*

> About eight days after this conversation, he took Peter, John, and James with him and went up into the hills to pray. And while he was praying the appearance of his face changed and his clothes became dazzling white. Suddenly there were two men talking with him; these were Moses and Elijah, who appeared in glory and spoke of his departure, the destiny he was to fulfill in Jerusalem. Meanwhile Peter and his companions had been in a deep sleep; but when they awoke, they saw his glory and the two men who stood beside him. And as these were moving away from Jesus, Peter said to him, "Master, how good it is that we are here! Shall we make three shelters, one for you, one for Moses, and one for Elijah?"; but he spoke without knowing what he was saying. The words were still on his lips when there came a cloud which cast a shadow over them; they were afraid as they entered the cloud, and from it came a voice: "This is my Son, my Chosen; listen to him." When the voice had spoken, Jesus was seen to be alone. The disciples kept silence and at that time told nobody anything of what they had seen. (Luke 9:28-35)

In Luke's account, Christ Jesus again went up on a mountain to pray. Just as he had done immediately before calling the apostles to him, he "spent the night in prayer to God" (Luke 6:12). That first night of prayer had been followed by the calling of the Twelve, marking the first gathering of the apostles' intimate circle of destiny around Christ. "When day broke he called his disciples to him, and from among them he chose twelve and named them Apostles" (Luke 6:13). Now Christ led three of these apostles up Mount Tabor (or, in Rudolf Frieling's translation, "brought them up" or "carried them up.")[79] There his divine nature, his "glory," was to reveal itself to this small, pathbreaking, human community. "What the disciples were allowed to see up there on the mountain was an experience that actually belongs to the future, an anticipation of something that illuminated their souls as if in the here-and-now."[80]

Christ's transfiguration began while he was praying. "*While he was praying, as a result of his praying*, the process of transfiguration began."[81] "And while he was praying, the appearance of his face changed..." (Luke 9:29). Matthew writes: "And in their presence he was transfigured; his face shone like the sun, and his clothes became white as the light" (Matthew 17:1-2). Out of the sphere of the sun, Christ Jesus' initial metamorphosis (a revelation of his sun spirituality and the reality that he was the Christ—or, in Peter's words, "God's Messiah") became perceptible to the disciples. As a result of his praying and the beginning of the transformation it initiated, his clothes became gleaming white from within. "His clothes became dazzling white" (Luke 9:29; Mark 9:3). "Suddenly there were two men talking with him; these were Moses and Elijah, who appeared in glory and spoke of his departure, the destiny he was to fulfill in Jerusalem" (Luke 9:31). Like Christ himself, Moses and Elijah revealed themselves to the disciples in their radiant "glory" (Greek *doxa*), in the light of revelation, as they talked with him. "*And they saw Moses and Elijah appear, conversing with him*" Matthew 17:3). The spirit beings, the individualities, of these long-dead figures appeared to the disciples' suprasensory perception—Moses and Elijah, in their active historical role as mediators between past and future:

> In the old covenant, Moses links back to primal beginnings. He beholds the genesis and receives the law that

will keep the world on course as creation intends. In contrast, Elijah was felt to be the genius of prophethood; surrounded by flames of eschatology and apocalypse, he points to the future. Moses' light-filled aura, therefore, contains aspects of the "*doxa* of the Father," whereas the aura of Elijah, as one of the Holy Spirit's angelic messengers, contains aspects of the "*doxa* of the Holy Spirit." Between these two figures stands Christ the Son, in his own *doxa*, although its full, exalted majesty is still to be achieved (through the culmination of the great Mystery on Golgotha).[82]

Moses and Elijah spoke with Christ about the impending Mystery of Golgotha, "the destiny he was to fulfill in Jerusalem" (Luke 9:31).

The disciples Peter, James, and John were struggling to maintain consciousness and were therefore capable of perceiving this revelation only to a rather limited extent. "Meanwhile Peter and his companions had been in a deep sleep; but when they awoke, they saw his glory [*doxa*] and the two men who stood beside him" (Luke 9:32). The disciples' spirit-eyes were "heavy," as they would also be before Christ's arrest (Mark 14:40), but at this point they did not fail Christ completely. "In such bright moments of higher consciousness, the disciples, struggling against stupor, nonetheless perceived his *doxa*."[83] A week after his announcement in Caesarea Philippi, they saw Christ in the "Kingdom of God."

"And as these were moving away from Jesus, Peter said to him, 'Master, how good it is that we are here! Shall we make three shelters, one for you, one for Moses, and one for Elijah?'; but he spoke without knowing what he was saying." Again Simon Peter gives expression to a power of temptation, but Christ rejects Peter's spontaneous effort to make the light-filled spirit phenomenon permanent. "The Christ does not allow the light-blessed transfiguration to fade away prematurely."[84]

Instead, it is confirmed by the full authority of the divinity. "A voice called out from the cloud: *'This is my Son, my Beloved, on whom my favor rests'*" (Matthew 17:5). As at the Baptism in the Jordan, the divine voice could be heard through inspired perception, but this time not only by Christ and John the Baptist, but also by three of the disciples. "This voice from heaven we ourselves heard; when it came we were with him on the sacred mountain," Peter wrote later, recalling the event (2 Peter 1:18).

The divine voice concludes with the command, "Listen to him" (Matthew 17:6, Mark 9:8, Luke 9:35). "The disciples are told to be receptive and ready to receive him as the Word itself in the full revelation of his being."[85] The road to Golgotha, the impending mystery of death, and the events after Easter required enhanced devotion from the disciples, and further growth with regard to spiritual understanding as a reality in their own existence. This is indicated by Christ's words in Caesarea Philippi: "If anyone wishes to be a follower of mine, he must leave self behind; he must take up his cross and come with me. Whoever cares for his own safety is lost; but if a man will let himself be lost for my sake, he will find his true self" (Matthew 16:24-25).

According to Matthew's account, Peter, James, and John reacted with fear. "At the sound of the voice the disciples fell on their faces in terror" (Matthew 17:6). This time Christ offered them support. "Jesus then came up to them, touched them, and said, 'Stand up; do not be afraid.' And when they raised their eyes they saw no one, but only Jesus" (Matthew 17:8). Christ touched his disciples only twice—at the washing of the feet on the evening of Maundy Thursday, and here on Mount Tabor, half a year earlier. The disciples were meant to find the path of consciousness together with Christ Jesus, through their own uprightness and fortitude: "Stand up; do not be afraid." Of necessity, however, this path led to death, to the events of the Passion. As Christ had first announced to them in Caesarea Philippi, he would "be put to death and…raised again on the third day."

The descent from Mount Tabor took place in silence. "In Luke's account, the Transfiguration as suprasensory perception of a mystery is sealed with the disciples' reverent silence as they set out down Mount Tabor."[86] According to Matthew and Mark, Christ swears the three disciples to silence: "Jesus enjoined them not to tell anyone of the vision until the Son of Man had been raised from the dead" (Matthew 17:9). Peter, James, and John were to keep the experience of the Transfiguration and Christ's conversation with Moses and Elijah to themselves until his reawakening or *resurrection*. "He enjoined them not to tell anyone what they had seen until the Son of Man had *risen from the dead*" (Mark 9:9). Mark continues:

> They seized upon those words and discussed among themselves what this "rising from the dead" could mean. And they put a question to him. "Why do our teachers say that Elijah must come first?" He replied, "Yes, Elijah does come first to set everything right. Yet how is it that the scriptures say of the Son of Man that he is to endure great sufferings and to be treated with contempt? However, I tell you, Elijah has already come and they have worked their will upon him, as the scriptures say of him." (Mark 9:10-13)

Matthew's account of the descent from Mount Tabor, which set the course toward the events on Golgotha, Christ's earthly Passion, is similar but ends with the words:

> "But I tell you that Elijah has already come, and they failed to recognize him, and they worked their will upon him; and in the same way the Son of Man is to suffer at their hands." *Then the disciples understood that he meant John the Baptist.* (Matthew 17:13)

In Matthew's account, on one previous occasion, long ago, while John was in prison, Christ had already spoken to his disciples about the mystery of the Baptist's being and reincarnation and his existence as Elijah:

> I tell you this: never has there appeared on earth a mother's son greater than John the Baptist, and yet the least in the kingdom of Heaven is greater than he. Ever since the coming of John the Baptist the kingdom of Heaven has been subjected to violence and violent men are seizing it. For all the prophets and the Law foretold things to come until John appeared, and John is the destined Elijah, *if you will but accept it. If you have ears, then hear.* (Matthew 11:11-15)

Now, however, after their experiences on Mount Tabor and with their consciousness at least partially awakened, the disciples Peter, James, and John were able to "accept" Christ's statement about Elijah-John; they were "receptive and ready to receive" Christ's word, as commanded by the divine voice (*"Listen to him!"*) they had perceived through inspiration. That the individuality of the Baptist accompanied them on their way as their "group soul," however, was by no means clear to them, and they were alienated by and opposed to the path that lay before Christ, even though they discussed his explanations among themselves. "They seized upon those words and discussed among themselves what this 'rising from the dead' could mean." (Mark 9:10). The events on Mount Tabor were a milestone on the road to the Mystery of Golgotha and a further test of the disciple's consciousness, at least for a small, select group of them.

*

Rudolf Steiner referred to these events as the "Mystery on Mount Tabor."[87] Even in early lectures, he indicated that in the four Gospels, mountain topography is always associated with intimate esoteric teachings; that is, with the innermost aspect of the Christ's proclamation. "The keywords 'on the mountain' signal that the master is leading his pupils deep within, where he will present his most intimate teachings."[88] "'Mountain' means the mystery places where close confidantes are instructed."[89] On October 3, 1905, in Berlin, Steiner said:

> "On the mountain" means deep within or "in the Mystery." As such, therefore, the Sermon on the Mount must be interpreted not as a sermon to the masses but as intimate instruction given to the disciples, and the Transfiguration on the mountain must also understood similarly.[90]

Years later, in one of his Gospel cycles, Rudolf Steiner emphasized:

> On the "mountain" he appointed the Twelve for the first time; that is, in an esoteric training session, he assigned them their esoteric mission. On the mountain is also where his esoteric Transfiguration took place.[91]

The so-called Sermon on the Mount was a forceful appeal to the "I"-force of the apostolic community as a whole. "The spirit of the Sermon on the Mount is entirely inspired by the new impulse of human 'I'-ness."[92] Christ had already included three individualities in the circle of disciples in the awakening of Jairus' daughter (cf. Luke 8:51; Mark 5:37).[93] For them, the Transfiguration on Mount Tabor signified "initiation of a higher sort."[94] Steiner described Simon, James, and John as the three disciples *"most receptive"* to the Christ-Power.[95] These three were "predestined to be introduced to the deeper secrets of the Mystery of Golgotha" and to reach devachan, a higher level of knowledge of the spiritual world.[96]

> Christ Jesus was to initiate his disciples (that is, those especially suited for it) in a very specific way that enabled them

to actually see (not merely through imagination, as if in astral images) and even hear what was happening in spiritual worlds. This ascent into spirit would then allow them to seek out Christ Jesus in the spiritual worlds, whom they knew as a personality on the physical plane. They were to become clairvoyant in realms higher than the astral plane. Not all of them were capable of this. It was possible only for those most receptive to the power radiating from the Christ; that is, the three disciples Peter, James, and John, as they are called in the Matthew Gospel. This Gospel tells us how Christ took these three disciples, the ones he influenced most, to a place where he could lead them up above the astral plane into devachan. There they could behold the spiritual archetype of Christ Jesus himself. Then, to understand his spiritual context, they also beheld the archetypes of two related beings. They saw the ancient prophet Elijah, who had also been reincarnated as the forerunner of Christ Jesus, John the Baptist. (This scene took place after John's beheading, when he was already in the spiritual world.) They also saw Moses, Christ's spiritual forerunner. These three selected disciples could see the three figures only when they had been led to the level of spiritual (not merely astral) beholding. The Matthew Gospel makes it clear that they had actually ascended into devachan, by recounting specifically that they not only beheld the Christ in his sun-power (the Gospel specifically says *"and his face shone like the sun"*) but they were also aware of the conversation among the three figures. Thus they must have ascended into devachan, because they heard the three converse.[97]

Peter, James, and John were to acquire deeper insight not only into the being of Christ, but also into his connection to his spiritual forerunners and the spiritual history of humanity's evolution, of which they themselves, as Christ's intimate pupils, were part. "In a way, the disciples were gradually being led to a new understanding of humanity's evolution, and the most suitable among them proved to be Peter, James, and John."[98] On Mount Tabor, in spiritual beholding or "clear moments of higher consciousness," Peter, James, and John stood outside of time and space.[99] They beheld not only the transformed, transfigured Christ but also Moses and Elijah, whose spiritual and spiritual-historical significance for the Christ Mystery Rudolf Steiner discussed in great detail. At the end of his lengthy explanation in Basel on September 22, 1912, he said, "Here we have coming together the spirituality of all of the Earth stage of evolution, of everything that streamed upward through the Jewish bloodline, and culminated in the Levites. Before us stands the soul of Phinehas, son of Eleazar, son of Aaron; before us stands the one who enacted the Mystery of Golgotha. How the forces, the spiritual currents, merge—that was what was to appear in imaginative cognition before the three candidates for initiation, the disciples Peter, James, and John. Above, the three cosmic powers on the mountain; below, the three to be initiated into these great cosmic secrets."[100] "The name Elijah means "way of God," the goal. *El*, meaning God, is also contained in Elohim, Gabriel, Michael, Raphael, and Bel (or Baal). The name Moses represents the truth; Moses is the esoteriv designation for truth. Jesus means life; Christ himself, standing in the middle, is life. The way, the truth, and the life—inscribed as if in words of steel in their minds."[101] Speaking elsewhere about the insight into reincarnation that was revealed to the three disciples during their descent from the mountain, Rudolf Steiner said:

> Through their master, these three disciples were to acquire even higher cognition than the others. In their experience up on the mountain, in particular, they were to become convinced that the Christ really was the living Word, the Word become flesh. To this end, he revealed himself in spirituality that transcends space and time; in spirituality that is entirely present, and knows no past or future. The past manifests in

the beings of Elijah and Moses, who appear alongside Jesus' "present." Now the disciples believe in God the Spirit. But they say, "It is written that Elijah will appear before the Christ, proclaiming his coming." Now read the Gospel; these are the actual words that follow the event I have described, and they are highly significant: "Elijah has come, but they did not recognize him and worked their will upon him." "Elijah has come"; let us keep these words in mind. And then the Gospel continues, "The disciples realized that he had been talking about John the Baptist." Earlier, Jesus had said to them, "Tell no one what you have experienced today until the Son of Man has risen from the dead." Here we are introduced to a mystery. Christ found only three disciples worthy of experiencing it. And what is this mystery? He told them that John is the reincarnated Elijah.

In the mystery temples, reincarnation had been taught down through the ages. Christ conveyed this same esoteric theosophical teaching to his trusted disciples. They were to become convinced of the truth of reincarnation, but they were also to acquire the living word this conviction inspires and enlivens. First they needed direct knowledge of the resurrection of the spirit. Having that, they were to go out into the whole world and strike in the simple hearts of others the sparks that had been kindled in their own hearts. This initiation was one of the parables Christ gave and explained to his trusted companions.[102]

At the same time, Rudolf Steiner pointed out that the disciples Peter, James, and John were able to follow and participate in the Mount Tabor mystery only to a very limited extent. "The disciples were called to this cosmic conversation up above the earth, on the mountain top, *but did not understand it.*"[103] Their consciousness was only very briefly able to achieve the level of such an event, which they could not truly grasp. "They fell asleep immediately, torn out of their physical and etheric bodies by the force of the event."[104] In spite of their having traveled with Christ for the past two years, the out-of-body state as a prerequisite to mystery vision was only very partially available to the three disciples. Rudolf Steiner said that they were therefore in no position to grasp and internalize Christ's announcement of impending events on Golgotha. "The Transfiguration was intended as a first step in this direction, but it also revealed that the disciples were initially not capable of fully receiving the Christ Principle."[105]

Immediately after their descent from Mount Tabor, Christ and the three disciples met the child the disciples had not been able to cure. Distressed at their failure, Christ promptly healed the boy. "The Christ acknowledges their very preliminary attempts, saying, 'I will need to remain with you for a long time before your forces will also be able to flow into other people.' And then he healed the boy the disciples had not be able to cure." Immediately after this healing, still at the foot of the mountain, Christ mentions his impending death to his disciples for the second time:

> Amid the general wonder and admiration at all he was doing, Jesus said to his disciples, "What I now say is for you: ponder my words. The Son of Man is to be given up into the power of men." (Luke 9:43-44)

"*Hear him!*" said the divine voice on the mountain of the Transfiguration. Once again, however, Christ's announcement of suffering to come ("ponder my words") exceeds the disciples' understanding; they were not yet "learners in the kingdom of Heaven" (Matthew 13:52).

> But they did not understand this saying ["The Son of Man is to be given up into the power of men"]; it had been hidden from them, so that they should not grasp its meaning, and they were afraid to ask him about it. (Luke 9:45)

> But they did not understand what he said, and were afraid to ask. (Mark 9:32)

According to the Luke Gospel account, Christ then set out on the road to Jerusalem, heading for the "outcome" he intended to fulfill.

> As the time approached when he was to be taken up to heaven, he set his face resolutely toward Jerusalem. (Luke 9:51)

The road to Golgotha

3.
Gethsemane and Golgotha

"Can I make the souls of at least my selected disciples rise to a level that allows them to share my experience of all that must happen as the Mystery of Golgotha approaches?"

This was the question the Christ-Soul confronted [in Gethsemane].

— Rudolf Steiner[107]

I̲n̲ ̲t̲h̲e̲ ̲c̲o̲u̲r̲s̲e̲ ̲o̲f̲ ̲t̲h̲e̲ ̲t̲h̲r̲e̲e̲ ̲y̲e̲a̲r̲s̲, the disciples' understanding of the Mystery of Christ and the Mystery of Golgotha, their "learning in the kingdom of Heaven," had to overcome many obstacles, and awakened only gradually and incompletely. Nonetheless, Christ was an intense presence in the inner circle of his pupils; this relationship and their community evolved through different phases related to the ever-deepening incarnation of the Christ Being into the body of Jesus. In his lectures on the Fifth Gospel, Rudolf Steiner said:

> As [Christ Jesus] moved through the countryside, his effect on those around him was unique. And because he was the Christ Being, for the apostles, the community of disciples, it was as if he was not merely in his own body. When he walked the countryside in the company of his disciples, one or the other of them sometimes felt Christ's presence in his own soul, even if they were walking side by side. Some of them felt the presence of the being belonging to Christ Jesus as if in their own souls, and they then began to speak words that only Christ Jesus himself could actually utter. As this group traveled and addressed the public, the one speaking was certainly not always Christ Jesus himself but sometimes one of the disciples, because he shared everything with them, including his wisdom.
>
> I must confess to being highly astonished when I realized, for example, that in the conversation with the Sadducees as recounted by the Mark Gospel, Christ Jesus spoke not out of the body of Jesus but through one of the disciples, although of course the Christ was the one speaking. It was a common phenomenon that when Christ Jesus left the group, as he sometimes did, he remained among them.

Either he walked with them in spirit while he was far away, or only his etheric body was actually among them, walking the countryside with them. It was often impossible to distinguish whether he had his physical body with him, so to speak, or whether only his ether body appeared there.

This was the nature of Jesus of Nazareth's interaction with the disciples and with some of the people from the masses once he had become Christ Jesus. As I have already pointed out, he himself certainly experienced that although the Christ Being was initially relatively independent of the body of Jesus of Nazareth, he gradually and increasingly came to resemble it. As life went on, the Christ became bound more closely to the body of Jesus of Nazareth. In his final year, his connection to this body, which meanwhile had become infirm, was a source of great pain to him. Nonetheless, the Christ, now traveling with a great band of followers, continued to leave his body. On any given occasion, one or the other of the apostles might speak, and people believed the speaker to be Christ Jesus (or not, as the case might be). As long as this intimate community traveled together, Christ spoke through them all.

The Pharisees and Jewish scholars can be heard conversing among themselves, saying, "Of course we could arbitrarily seize one member of this group and kill him, to scare the people off, but we might easily get the wrong one because they all speak alike. That would do no good at all, because the real Christ Jesus might still be there. We must get the right one!" Only the disciples themselves, who had grown closer to him, could tell which one of them he was, and they certainly did not tell the enemy.[108]

In another lecture in the Fifth Gospel cycle, Rudolf Steiner reported that Christ spoke *through* individual disciples:

When we behold the traveling band of disciples, we sometimes get the very distinct, conscious impression that the physical body of Jesus of Nazareth is among them, especially when Christ Jesus seeks out a lonely place with his disciples. But we also often get the impression that the bodily personality of Jesus of Nazareth is far away, although the disciples are conscious of the Christ Being's presence among them. The strange fact, however, is that this being could speak through each of the disciples in turn. Moreover, while one or the other of them was speaking to the masses, his entire physiognomy appeared transformed, as if hallowed. One among them was always transfigured, and as time went on, it was always a different one. Awareness grew that someone was inciting the people and divulging matters that the leading Jews of the time did not want known, but they did not know who it was. He spoke sometimes through one, sometimes through another. The akashic record tells us that this is why Judas' betrayal was required.

I must confess to having been puzzled as to why the betrayal was really necessary. Why did Judas have to kiss Christ to identify him? This seemed a very strange way to communicate until I realized that it was really impossible to tell which one of them he was, because he could speak through any one of them, so even when he was present among them in body, that body was not recognizable. Depending on which one he was speaking through, any one of them could be taken for him. Hence the need for someone who knew Christ Jesus was really present among them in body to tell the Jews, "This is the one!" before they could seize him.[109]

Rudolf Steiner said that the disciples were deeply moved by the Christ, yet unable to completely penetrate his words (or their task) in their state of day-consciousness. Christ was able to speak *through* them, transforming himself into each of the disciples through a process of inspiration. "Then his face changed; even to outer view, his physiognomy became very different. Meanwhile, whenever it happened that one of the disciples spoke the magnificent words of Christ, the actual outer appearance of Christ Jesus also changed, and he looked like the simplest one in their circle. This happened over and over again."[110] His closest disciples were so intimately connected to the Christ that "his life was not separate from theirs, so to speak." The Christ Being increasingly indwelt not only the physical nature of Jesus, but also the innermost being of his pupils, the chosen disciples. "Christ spoke sometimes through one, sometimes through another of these pupils; he indwelt the others in this circle through their intimate association."[111]

> He indwelt the disciples with such force, and the face of the disciple through whom he spoke was transformed to such an extent, that the listening masses had the feeling, this one is the master; while the Christ himself appeared diminished and quite ordinary. Thus he spoke first through one, then through another as they moved through the countryside. *This was the secret of his activity toward the end of the three years.*[112]

*

Not far from Jericho in Judea, as they were approaching Jerusalem, Christ announced his impending suffering to the disciples for the third time (the first two being the words he spoke near Caesarea Philippi and then at the foot of Mount Tabor). "They were on the road, going up to Jerusalem, Jesus leading the way; and ... those who followed behind were afraid. He took the Twelve aside and began to tell them what was to happen to him. 'We are now going to Jerusalem,' he said; 'and the Son of Man will be given up to the chief priests and the doctors of the law; they will condemn him to death and hand him over to the foreign power. He will be mocked and spat upon, flogged and killed; and three days afterward he will rise again'" (Mark 10:32-34). "All that was written by the prophets will come true for the Son of Man" (Luke 18:31) in passing through the Mystery of Golgotha. On the way to Jerusalem, according to Matthew, Jesus mentioned not only the "cross" each one had to bear, but also his own eminent *crucifixion*. "And they will condemn him to death and hand him over to the foreign power, to be mocked and flogged and crucified, and on the third day he will be raised to life again" (Matthew 20:19). Again, however, the disciples did not understand the Lord. Their consciousness did not rise to his level; they were at once close to him and far away. "But they understood nothing of all this; they did not grasp what he was talking about; its meaning was concealed from them" (Luke 18:34). Rudolf Frieling writes of this passage in Luke: "Their lack of understanding is emphasized more radically than ever before. The disciples did not 'grasp' it; in Greek, 'they did not bring it together.' Their thoughts could not grasp it; they could not unite undergoing death and being resurrected in a single view. They could not reconcile the entire situation with their previous conceptions of Christ; it remained 'concealed from them.' And, finally, the ceremonial word for 'cognition,' *ginoskein*, is used, but in the negative: they understood nothing."[113]

Jesus spent the nights of Holy Week on the Mount of Olives. "His days were given to teaching in the temple; and then he would leave the city and spend the night on the hill called Olivet" (Luke 21:37). There, on Tuesday, he spoke to the three disciples who had been with him on Mount Tabor (as well as to Andrew) about his Second Coming in an apocalyptic time characterized by destruction. "But in those days, after that distress, the sun will be darkened, the moon will not give her light; the stars will come falling from the sky, the celestial powers will be shaken. Then they will see the Son of Man coming in the clouds with great power and glory" (Mark 13:24-26). Christ's speech to the three disciples who had experienced a "higher initiation" on Mount Tabor ends with an appeal to their power of consciousness, an appeal to "be alert, be wakeful." On Mount Tabor, the "eyes" of Peter, James, and John had "grown heavy," although they awoke intermittently. Now Christ says to them emphatically, including the entire circle of disciples, "Be alert, be wakeful. You do not know when the moment comes…. If [the master] comes suddenly, he must not find you asleep. And what I say to you, I say to everyone: *Keep awake!*" (Matthew 13:33-37).

Two days later, during the Last Supper in the Cenacle of the house of the Essenes, Christ performed for his disciples the transubstantiation of bread and wine, the real and symbolic sacrifice of his being. *"Take this; this is my body….This is my blood"* (Mark 14:22-24). Emil Bock writes:

> His soul surrenders itself and streams into the bread and wine. In the twilight of the room bread and wine are enveloped with a shining sun-aura. Inasmuch as they become body and blood of the Christ soul, they become body and blood of the Sun-Spirit himself. All the Sun-mysteries of antiquity were but prophecy; at this moment they grow into fulfillment. In the transition from the blood offerings of the past to the bloodless offering of bread and wine, the whole idea of sacrifice has changed. Ancient sacrifices were always material offerings. Now the sacrifice of the soul is founded, and there begins the true tradition of inner sacrifice. The lunar sacrifices of antiquity are at an end; the solar sacrifice of Christianity comes into being. Christianity, the true sun religion, dawns in this evening hour.[114]

Before the transformation of bread and wine, the omen and substance of Christ's imminent sacrifice on Golgotha, Christ had turned to his disciples in a unique way in the washing of the feet, an "entirely new ceremonial Mystery-sacrament."[115]

> During supper, Jesus, well aware that the Father had entrusted everything to him, and that he had come from

God and was going back to God, rose from the table, laid aside his garments, and taking a towel, tied it round him. Then he poured water into a basin, and began to wash his disciples' feet and to wipe them with the towel.

When it was Simon Peter's turn, Peter said to him, "You, Lord, washing my feet?" Jesus replied, "You do not understand now what I am doing, but one day you will." Peter said, "I will never let you wash my feet." "If I do not wash you," Jesus replied, "you are not in fellowship with me." "Then, Lord," said Simon Peter, "not my feet only; wash my hands and head as well!" (John 13:3-9)

"You do not understand now what I am doing, but one day you will." The consciousness of the disciples was still far removed from the true level of events, and yet Christ did what needed to be done. He prepared the disciples in a ritual cleansing of the community ("I have set you an example: you are to do as I have done for you") and in the subsequent communion with the bread and wine. Then, after Judas left, he spoke to them in the great farewell discourses that John has passed down to us. Emil Bock writes:

> These words are the body and blood of Christ in a still higher degree than the bread and wine. The soul of Christ gives itself to the souls of the disciples, who are only able to receive it as yet as though in a dream. Only John, who lies at the breast of Jesus and listens to the speaking heart of Christ, is able in his Gospel to preserve for humankind a reflection of this moment.[116]

Christ began his words to the disciples with a repeated announcement of his impending death. "My children, for a little longer I am with you; then you will look for me, and, as I told the Jews, I tell you now, where I am going you cannot come" (John 13:33). Peter then inquired, "'Lord, where are you going?'

Jesus replied, 'Where I am going you cannot follow me now, but one day you will.' Peter said, 'Lord, why cannot I follow you now? I will lay down my life for you.' Jesus answered, 'Will you indeed lay down your life for me? I tell you in very truth, before the cock crows you will have denied me three times'" (John 13:36-38). In spite of Christ's predictions of his sufferings, his disciples still do not understand his subsequent words about going home to the Father and later coming to them again:

> "Set your troubled hearts at rest. Trust in God always; trust also in me. There are many dwelling-places in my Father's house; if it were not so I should have told you; for I am going there on purpose to prepare a place for you. And if I go and prepare a place for you, I shall come again and receive you to myself, so that where I am you may be also; and my way there is known to you." Thomas said, "Lord, we do not know where you are going, so how can we know the way?" Jesus replied, "I am the way; I am the truth and I am life; no one comes to the Father except by me. If you knew me, you would know my Father too. From now on you do know him; you have seen him." Phillip said to him, "Lord, show us the Father and we ask no more."
>
> Jesus answered, "Have I been all this time with you, Philip, and you still do not know me? Anyone who has seen me has seen the Father. Then how can you say, 'Show us the father?' Do you not believe that I am in the Father, and the Father in me? I am not myself the source of the words I speak to you; it is the Father who dwells in me doing his own work. Believe me when I say that I am in the Father and the Father in me, or else accept the evidence of the deeds themselves." (John 14:1-11)

Then Christ spoke of his connection to the community of disciples and of how they would continue to act out of the inner substance of his being. He spoke to them about their future *after* Pentecost, when their spirit-knowledge would be complete and they would embark on their apostolate, their work in the world, in community with him:

> "In truth, in very truth I tell you, he who has faith in me will do what I am doing; and he will do greater things still because I am going to the Father. Indeed anything you ask in my name I will do, so that the Father may be glorified in the Son. If you ask anything in my name I will do it."
>
> "If you love me you will obey my commands; and I will ask the Father, and he will give you another to be your Advocate, who will be with you forever, the Spirit of truth. The world cannot receive him, because the world neither sees nor knows him; but you know him, because he dwells with you and is in you. I will not leave you bereft; I am coming back to you. In a little while, the world will see me no longer, but you will see me; because I live, you too will live; then you will know that I am in my Father, and you in me and I in you. The man who has received my commands and obeys them—he it is who loves me; and he who loves me will be loved by my father; and I will love him and disclose myself to him." Judas asked him (the other Judas, not Iscariot), "Lord, what can have happened, that you mean to disclose yourself to us alone, and not to the world?"
>
> Jesus replied, "Anyone who loves me will heed what I say; then my Father will love him, and we will come to him and make our dwelling with him; but he who does not love me does not heed what I say. And the word you hear is not mine: it is the word of the Father who sent me. I have told you all this while I am still here with you; but your Advocate, the Holy Spirit, whom the Father will send in my name, will teach you everything, and will call to mind all that I have told you." (John 14:12-26)

Christ then asked the disciples to keep his words alive in them and to dwell in his love, to act in his name and spirit. "If you heed my commandments, you will dwell in my love, as I have heeded my Father's commands and dwell in his love" (John 15:10). He emphasized his mystical, spiritual union with their community: "I am the vine, and you the branches" (John 15:5). He called the disciples his friends and told them of his love for them. "As the Father has loved me, so I have loved you" (John 15:9). He also spoke to them, however, about the need to arrive at cognition in *freedom*. "I call you servants no longer; a servant does not know what his master is about. I have called you friends, because I have disclosed to you everything that I heard from my Father" (John 15:15). He challenges them to do fruitful work in future through their connection to him. "...that the Father may give you all that you ask in my name" (John 15:16). Their discipleship will actually only be established through this *future* work. "Thus will my Father be revealed, that you bear fruit in plenty and so become my disciples" (John 15:8). Continuing what he said in Caesarea Philippi, Christ warns the disciples that they too must tread the path of suffering, martyrdom, and death:

> "They will ban you from the synagogue; indeed, the time is coming when anyone who kills you will suppose that he is performing a religious duty. They will do these things because they do not know either the Father or me. I have told you all this so that when the time comes for it to happen, you may remember my warning. I did not tell you this at first because then I was with you; but now I am going away to Him who sent me. None of you asks me, 'Where are you going?' Yet you are plunged into grief because of what I have told you. Nevertheless I tell you the truth: it is for your good that I am leaving you. If I do not go, your Advocate will not come; whereas if I go, I will send him to you. (John 16:1-7)

The disciples will be supported by the "spirit of truth" the Father sends to them through Christ:

> "However, when he comes who is the Spirit of truth, he will guide you into all the truth; for he will not speak on his own authority, but will tell only what he hears; and he will make known to you the things that are coming. He will glorify me, for everything that he makes known to you he will draw from what is mine. All that the Father has is mine, and that is why I said, 'Everything that he makes known to you he will draw from what is mine.'
> A little while, and you see me no more; again a little while, and you will see me." (John 16:13-16)

*

The meaning of Christ's words remained unclear to the disciples:

> Some of his disciples said to one another, "What does he mean by this: 'A little while, and you will not see me, and again a little while, and you will see me,' and by this: 'Because I am going to my Father'?" So they asked, "What is this 'little while' that he speaks of? *We do not know what he means.*" (John 16:17-18)

Jesus experienced their inner questioning, even without words:

> Jesus knew that they were wanting to question him, and said, "Are you discussing what I said: 'A little while, and you will not see me, and again a little while, and you will see me'?" (John 16:19)

He foretold that the disciples would feel sorrow at his death, but experience joy and understanding after his resurrection and the subsequent events of Pentecost. "I shall see you again, and then you will be joyful, and no one shall rob you of your joy. When that day comes you will ask nothing of me" (John 16:22-23). Then he continued:

> "In very truth I tell you, if you ask the Father for anything in my name, he will give it you. So far you have asked nothing in my name. Ask and you will receive, that your joy may be complete.
> Till now I have been using figures of speech; a time is coming when I shall no longer use figures, but tell you of the Father in plain words. When that day comes you will make your request in my name, and I do not say that I shall pray to the Father for you, for the Father loves you himself, because you have loved me and believed that I came from God. I came from the Father and have come into the world. Now I am leaving the world and going back to the Father." (John 16:23-28)

As John reports, the effect of these words (or of the discourse as a whole) was to illumine the disciples' consciousness. Christ promised this intimate community that in future he would tell them about the Father directly, without using images. "Till now I have been using figures of speech; a time is coming when I shall no longer use figures, but tell you of the Father in plain words." In a certain sense, however, this future had already dawned in the disciples' inner experience:

> His disciples said, "Why, this is plain speaking; this is no figure of speech. We are certain now that you know everything, and do not need to be questioned; because of this we believe that you have come from God." (John 16:29-30)

In his profession of faith at Caesarea Philippi, which emerged from the deepest levels of his being, Peter acknowledged the Christ as coming from God, as "God's Messiah." Now the disciples as a community reiterate Peter's words. Rudolf Steiner tells us that they took another step toward awakening in Christ-consciousness through their (at least temporary) understanding of the Father and of the Son who was heading toward death in order to be resurrected. Steiner said:

> By this point in time, his pupils have become increasingly mature and believe they are ready to hear the truth directly, without proverbs or parables. Christ foretells a time when he will speak to them without parables. The apostles want to hear the all-important name of the one who sent him into the world. "So far you have asked nothing in my name. Ask and you will receive, that your joy may be complete. Till now I have been using figures of speech; a time is coming when I shall no longer use figures, but tell you of the Father in plain words."
>
> We feel the time approaching when he will speak to his disciples about the Father. "When that day comes you will make your request in my name, and I do not say that I shall pray to the Father for you, for the Father loves you himself, because you have loved me and believed that I came from God. I came from the Father."
>
> Of course, he came from the Father in the Father's true form, not from any illusory manifestation of the Father. "I came from the Father and have come into the world. Now I am leaving the world and going back to the Father."
>
> Now the disciples have matured enough to recognize the world around them as the outer expression of the Father. It dawns on them that the most significant aspect of the outer world—where the maya or illusion of that world is strongest—is the expression of the Father; that is, that death is the name for the Father. That is what they realize; it must simply be interpreted correctly. "His disciples said to him, 'Why, this is plain speaking; this is no figure of speech. We are certain now that you know

everything, and do not need to be questioned; because of this we believe that you have come from God.' Jesus answered them, 'Now you believe. Look, the hour is coming, has indeed already come, when you will be scattered, each to his home, leaving me alone. But I am not alone, because the Father is with me. I have told you all this that you may find peace in me. In the world you will know fear; but be comforted, for I have overcome the world.'"

Did the disciples now know where he was going? Yes, from now on they knew that he was to be wedded to death. And then you read what he said to them after they had learned to understand the words "I came from death"—that is, from death in its true form, from the Life-Father—"and have come into the world. Now I am leaving the world and going to the Father." Then his disciples said, "Now we know that you know everything and do not need to be questioned; because of this we believe that you have come from God."

Now the disciples knew that death in its true form has its foundations in the divine Father-Spirit; that death as seen and felt by human beings is a deceptive error. This is how the Christ reveals to his disciples the name of death, which conceals the source of the most exalted life. The new Sun of Life could never have come about if death had not come into the world, and allowed itself to be overcome by the Christ. Thus death, seen in its true form, is the Father. And the Christ has come into the world because death has become a false image of the Father. The Christ has come to create a true image of the living Father God. The Son is the offspring who reveals his Father's true form. Truly, the Father has sent his son into the world to reveal the Father's true nature; that is, the eternal life that is concealed behind temporal death.[117]

*

"Christ concludes his farewell discourses at the Last Supper by turning in prayer to the Father God."[118] Looking "up to heaven" (John 17:1), turning toward the Father, toward the impending Mystery of Golgotha and the completion of the Transfiguration, he spoke the high priestly prayer for the future existence of the community of his disciples and their friends and companions:

> Father, the hour has come. Glorify thy Son, that the Son may glorify thee. For thou hast made him sovereign over all humankind, to give eternal life to all whom thou hast given him. This is eternal life: to know thee who alone art truly God, and Jesus Christ whom thou hast sent.
>
> I have glorified thee on earth by completing the work which thou gavest me to do; and now, Father, glorify me in thy own presence with the light of being which I had with thee before the world began.
>
> I have made thy name known to the men whom thou didst give me out of the world. They were thine, thou gavest them to me, and they have obeyed thy command. Now they know that all thy gifts have come to me from thee; for I have taught them all that I learned from thee, and they have received it: they know with certainty that I came from thee; they have had faith to believe that thou didst send me.
>
> I pray for them as single human beings; I am not praying for humankind in general but for those whom thou hast given me, because they belong to thee. All that is mine is thine, and what is thine is mine; and the light of my being shines in them.
>
> Now I am no longer in the earthly world, but they are still in the world and I am on my way to thee. Holy Father, protect by the power of thy name those whom thou hast given me, that they may be one as we are one. When I was with them, I protected by the power of thy name those whom thou hast given me, and kept them safe. Not one

of them has been lost except the son of iniquity, and thus Scripture was fulfilled.

And now I am coming to thee, but while I am still in the world I speak these words, so that my joy may fill their being. I have delivered thy word to them, and the world hates them because they are strangers in the world. I pray thee not to take them out of the world, but to keep them from the evil one. They are strangers in the world, as I am.

Consecrate them by the truth; thy word is truth. As thou hast sent me into the world, I have sent them into the world, and for their sake I now consecrate myself, that they too may be consecrated by the truth.

But it is not for them alone that I pray, but also for those who through their words put their faith in me; may they all be one: as thou, Father, art in me, and I in thee, so also may they be in us, that the world may believe that thou didst send me. The light of being that thou gavest to me I have given to them, that they may be one, as we are one; I in them and thou in me, may they be perfectly one. Then the world will learn that thou didst send me, that thou didst love them as thou didst love me.

Father, it is my will that these men, whom thou hast given me, may be with me where I am, so that they may behold the light of being that thou hast given me, because thou didst love me before the world began. O righteous Father, although the world does not know thee, I know thee, and these men know that thou didst send me. I made thy name known to them, and will make it known, so that the love thou hadst for me may be in them, and I may be in them. (John 17:1-26)

Then Christ, accompanied by his disciples, left for the garden of Gethsemane on the Mount of Olives, where he would be arrested.

*

Jesus then came with them to a place called Gethsemane. He said to them, "Sit here while I go over there to pray." He took with him Peter and the two sons of Zebedee. Anguish and agitation came over him, and he said to them, "My soul is deathly tired; stop here and stay awake with me." He went a few steps farther and threw himself on his face in prayer: "My Father, if it is possible, let this cup pass me by. Yet not as I will, but as thou wilt."

Then he came to the disciples and found them asleep; and he said to Peter, "Are you not strong enough to stay awake with me even for one hour? Stay awake and pray that you do not succumb to temptation. The spirit is willing, but the flesh is weak." So he went away a second time, and prayed: "My Father, if it is not possible for this cup to pass me by without my drinking it, thy will be done."

When he came back, he found them asleep again, for their eyes were heavy. So he left them and went away again; and he prayed the third time, using the same words as before.

Then he came to the disciples and said to them, "Still sleeping? Still taking your lease? The hour has come! The Son of Man will be delivered into the hands of sinners. Wake up, let us go. See, there is the one who has betrayed me."

While he was still speaking, Judas, one of the Twelve, appeared, and with him a great crowed armed with swords and cudgels, sent by the high priests and elders of the nation. (Matthew 26:36-47)

Gethsemane was the setting for "Christ's final retreat into prayer."[119] Here again, the three specially selected disciples who had been with him on Mount Tabor and participated in its mystery were overcome by sleep. There on the holy mountain they had awakened from stupor, and their consciousness had been illumined for brief periods, allowing them to participate as eyewitnesses. In Gethsemane, however, they failed to provide spiritual support for Christ Jesus; they did not pray with him in this decisive hour. Rudolf Frieling writes:

> During the Last Supper, the Christ surrendered his life forces to the disciples, but they failed by not finding the right answer to this sacrifice. Instead of closing the circle and helping him by standing by him as he struggled to remain in his broken body, they succumbed, their consciousness darkened, and left him alone one last time. The circle of the Twelve was broken when Judas went out into the night. Once in the garden, the Christ had to leave behind eight more disciples who, although they did not betray him, were in no way equal to the task of the hour. Only his three closest disciples were left. Leaving the others behind, he walked on into the garden with these three, but they too failed him.[120]

Following Rudolf Steiner's indications, Rudolf Frieling emphasizes that Christ is engaged in a real death struggle in the garden of Gethsemane. The crisis is extreme, and it is physical, not emotional. Luke, the physician, says "he was in agony,"; that is, in the throes of death (Luke 22:44).

In his lectures on the Fifth Gospel, Rudolf Steiner pointed out repeatedly that Christ's three years on earth were years of suffering for him:

> Increasingly, the Christ Being had to descend into and unite with the constitutional members of Jesus of Nazareth, but the union was complete only toward the end of the three years; actually, only during the Crucifixion just before his death on the cross. This process of uniting with the human body caused ever-increasing suffering. The all-embracing, universal Spirit Being of the Christ was able to unite with the body of Jesus of Nazareth only through unspeakable suffering that lasted three years.

We cannot wax sentimental when we behold this process, for the impression we receive from the spiritual world has nothing sentimental about it. Undoubtedly, no other impression compares to the suffering involved in the union of the Christ Being with the physical nature of Jesus of Nazareth. We learn to recognize what a god had to suffer so that humankind, grown old, could experience rejuvenation, so that human beings could become capable of taking full possession of the "I."[121]

On the bodily, physical plane, Steiner said, the Christ's three years of deepening incarnation after the Baptism in the Jordan corresponded to an ever-increasing death process:

There at the Jordan stands Jesus of Nazareth. His "I" separates from his physical body, his ether body or life body, and his astral body, and the macrocosmic Christ Being descends, taking possession of these three bodies and indwelling them until April 3 of the year 33, as we can determine. But that was a different life. Beginning already before the Baptism, Christ's life in the body of Jesus was a slow process of dying. With each elapsing phase in these three years of life, something more in the bodily sheaths of Jesus of Nazareth died off. These bodily garments slowly died off, so that after three years the body of Jesus of Nazareth was very close to becoming a corpse, held together only by the power of the macrocosmic Christ Being.

You must not imagine that this body indwelt by Christ Jesus (a year and a half after his baptism by John in the Jordan, for example) was like any other body. Any ordinary human soul would have felt it falling away, because it could be held together only by the mighty, macrocosmic being of the Christ. These three years were a constant, slow process of dying off. When the Mystery of Golgotha commenced, this body had reached its limits and was about to fall apart."[122]

Rudolf Frieling tells us that Christ's body was already close to death (in fact, in the throes of death) in Gethsemane. Death at that moment, however, would have been *premature* with regard to predestined events on Golgotha. "Here Christ struggles with death itself, not with fear of death. Dying prematurely would prevent the fulfillment of the divinely prescribed, destined ritual of Good Friday, up to and including the death on the cross."[123] According to Luke's account, Christ was literally torn from his disciples: "And he was torn away from them, about a stone's throw away..." (Luke 22:41). In place of the disciples who failed him, an angel stood by him in his existential struggle with death:

> And now there appeared to him an angel from heaven bringing him strength. As the agony of death came over him, he prayed the more urgently; and his sweat became drops of blood falling on the earth. (Luke 22:43-44)

According to Frieling, Christ did not pray to be spared on Golgotha. The satanic words uttered by Peter in Caesarea Philippi ("Heaven forbid! No, Lord, this shall never happen to you") did not fall from his lips. Rather, Christ prayed that he might survive until Golgotha, when the "divinely prescribed, destined ritual" would be completed. "When he prayed that death might pass him by, he was really praying for the strength to enact the sacrifice on Golgotha as it was 'predestined' to occur."[124] At the same time, however, Christ was ready to submit fully to the will of the Father: "Yet not my will but thine be done" (Luke 22:42). "In the agony of death, the Christ sees the approach of premature death as totally incomprehensible, thwarting the divine plan of destiny visible to his spirit eye until now. He struggles to accept this incomprehensible event, if in fact it is inevitable, as also coming from his Father."[125] With the help of the strength of the angel who stepped in to replace the disciples who failed him, Christ finally overcame the agony through his destined, willing submission to God. "...because of his humble submission his prayer was heard," Paul later writes in his Letter to the Hebrews (Hebrews 5:7-8).

The necessary course of events that culminate on Golgotha already includes both Judas' satanic or Ahrimanic betrayal (cf. John 13:2 and 14:27 and Luke 22:3), which originated in the inner circle of the disciples, and Christ's arrest in Gethsemane following his "final retreat into prayer."[126] Christ forbids his disciples, now awake again but spiritually only marginally present, from intervening with force of arms, and they finally take flight, avoiding the events of Golgotha. "Then the disciples all deserted him and ran away" (Mark 14:51). Hours later, Peter, who followed the band of soldiers at a distance, would deny his membership in Christ's inner circle of disciples three times in the courtyard of the high priest, breaking his earlier vow. Then Peter, too, utters the words "I do not know this man" (Mark 14:71) and "No, I am not" (Luke 22:58) when accused of being one of them. Rudolf Frieling, writing about this phrase "I am not," says, "In the Greek, *ouk eimi* means both 'it is not I' and 'I am not' in the sense of 'I do not exist.' Moreover, since the subject of the verb is dropped, it is actually more like 'not me.'"[127] Thus this phrase perfectly expresses Peter's state of largely extinguished "I"-consciousness.

*

In a lecture belonging to the larger context of the Fifth Gospel, Rudolf Steiner had this to say about what took place in the garden of Gethsemane (which also had been the setting for earlier instruction), and about the disciples' level of consciousness:

> Are the apostles, the chosen disciples, ready for this level of understanding? Have they recognized Christ Jesus as

the cosmic spirit? Have they recognized one among them as more than the person he appeared to be, surrounded by an aura through which cosmic forces and cosmic laws entered the earth? Have they understood?

The Gospels indicate that Christ Jesus expected this understanding of them. When the two sons of Zebedee approach him and ask to sit in state with him, one on his right and one on his left, he says, "You do not understand what you are asking. Can you drink the cup that I drink, or be baptized with the baptism I am baptized with?" (Mark 10:38). At first, the disciples aver that they can indeed do this, and this passage makes it clear that Christ Jesus expects it of them. From the apostles' perspective, there were now two possibilities. One was that the chosen disciples would really accompany Christ through all the events Golgotha, and the bond between them and Christ would remain intact until the Mystery of Golgotha was accomplished. That was one possible course of events, but the Mark Gospel, in particular, makes it clear that it did not happen. When Christ Jesus is taken captive, they all flee, and Peter, who had sworn that nothing could deter him, denies him three times before the cock crows twice. This is the apostles' perspective. But what does it look like from the Christ's perspective?

With all due humility, of course, let us find our way into the soul state of Christ Jesus, who attempted until the very end to maintain the bond that linked him to the souls of the apostles. To the extent available to us, let us view the further course of events through the soul of Christ. This soul must have asked a question of world-historical import: "Will I be able to raise the souls of at least these selected disciples to a level that allows them to accompany me through all the experiences leading up to the Mystery of Golgotha?" This is the question Christ's soul confronts. It is a magnificent moment when Peter, James, and John are led out to the Mount of Olives; the Christ will discover whether he can retain these chosen few. On the way, he grows anxious. My friends, are we allowed to believe that the Christ grew anxious before his death, before the Mystery of Golgotha? That he sweated blood on the Mount of Olives over the impending events of Golgotha? That would gain us little understanding of this Mystery. It may be theologically correct, but it does not make sense. Why is Christ sad? It goes without saying that he is not afraid of the cross. What he fears at this moment is that his companions will not endure the moment of decision: Will their souls be able to accompany him in experiencing all the events leading to the Crucifixion? What is to be decided here is whether they will remain awake, whether their state of consciousness will prove adequate to accompany him to the cross. This is the "cup" he sees approaching. He leaves them alone, asking them to remain "awake"; that is, in a state of consciousness in which they can share what he himself must experience. Then he goes on and prays, "Father, let this cup pass me by; but not my will, but thy will be done." This means, do not let me experience standing completely alone as the Son of Man; let the others accompany me. Then he comes back and finds them asleep; they have not been able to maintain the necessary state of consciousness. He makes a second attempt, and again they cannot maintain it. He tries yet a third time, and still they fail.

It was then clear to him that he stood there alone, that they would not accompany him on the way to the cross. The cup had not passed him by. He was destined to complete the deed as a lonely soul.

When the Mystery of Golgotha took place, the world did not yet understand this event. Not even the most carefully chosen few could remain steadfast to the extent needed.[128]

According to Rudolf Steiner, therefore, the central issue on that night in Gethsemane was not (entirely) either a psychological or physical struggle with death, but revolved around the disciples' ability to consciously participate in the coming events on Golgotha. The decisive point for Christ Jesus was whether the "bond" that had developed between him and the inner circle of disciples in the past three years could be maintained. "This soul must have asked a question of world-historical import: 'Will I be able to raise the souls of at least these selected disciples to a level that allows them to accompany me through all the experiences leading up to the Mystery of Golgotha?'" Peter, James, and John, who had participated (at least partially) in Christ's initial transfiguration on Mount Tabor, were also meant to witness the events of Golgotha with alert consciousness and maximum presence of mind and spirit. Having failed the Christ to a certain extent on Mount Tabor, these three, the "chosen few" among the disciples and thus pioneers of a human future, fail him completely in Gethsemane. In the end, in spite of having spent three years preparing his disciples, in spite of foretelling his sufferings, in spite of his shattering farewell discourses on Maundy Thursday, Christ had to perform the Mystery of Golgotha all alone, *as a lonely soul*.

*

In the Matthew and Mark Gospels, Christ says to the disciples at the end of the Last Supper: "You will all fall from your faith; for it stands written, 'I will strike the shepherd down and the sheep of his flock will be scattered'" (Matthew 26:31; Mark 14:27). John reports Christ's words as, "You are all to be scattered, each to his home, leaving me alone" (16:32). And in fact the disciples did all "scatter" after their Lord's arrest. With the exception of John, who had a specific role to play, none of the disciples witnessed what took place on Golgotha. Only the women (according to Mark) and a few friends of Christ (according to Luke) watched the Crucifixion "from a distance" (Mark 15:40-41; Luke 23:49); while the disciples (with the exception of John) were absent in both body *and* spirit. "They all scattered and ran away as the one they had followed until then set forth on his path of suffering."[129] On the cross of Golgotha, Christ surrendered his earthly life to the Father "as a lonely soul," without the support and involvement of the community of disciples with whom he had spent three years and whom he had warmly commended to the Father just one day earlier. "The light of being that thou gavest to me I have given to them, that they may be one, as we are one; I in them and thou in me, may they be perfectly one. Then the world will learn that thou didst send me, that thou didst love them as thou didst love me." In one lecture, Rudolf Steiner said:

> From everything we can reveal about the Christ Event, we see that the followers who had been drawn to the Christ during his lifetime became deeply confused when he met his end on the cross—a death that, at that time and place, was seen as the only possible atonement for the worst crimes against humanity. Admittedly, the death on the cross did not affect all of them as profoundly as it did Saul (soon to become Paul), who concluded that any man who died in this way could not possibly be the Messiah. But even if its effect on the other disciples was somewhat less negative, it is quite obvious that the Evangelists deliberately evoked the impression that in a certain sense, Christ Jesus lost all of his influence over the hearts of those around him through his ignominious death on the cross.[130]

*

At the foot of the cross, however, along with Jesus' mother Mary, stood the disciple John, whom Christ himself had initiated. According to Rudolf Steiner, this John was the resurrected

Lazarus and the "highest initiate" in the circle of disciples. "The disciple whom Jesus loved is also the highest initiate. He is the one who went through death and resurrection, awakened by the voice of Christ himself. John is Lazarus, raised from the grave after his initiation. *John experienced the death of Christ*."[131] At the Last Supper, when Christ foretold that he would soon be betrayed by a member of the group, the disciples turned to John for help. "The disciples looked at one another in bewilderment; whom could he be speaking of? One of them, the disciple he loved, was reclining close beside Jesus. So Simon Peter nodded to him and said, 'Ask who it is he means.' That disciple, as he reclined, leaned back close to Jesus and asked, 'Lord, who is it?'" (John 13:22-26). John, who was closest to the Christ, represents the heart organ in the circle of apostles. "What the heart is in the human body, John is among the twelve disciples."[132] John lived in the "Mystery of the Son."[133] On Golgotha, he stood at the cross with the Lord's mother.

The community of disciples had disbanded and the individuals "scattered," but shortly before his death on the cross Christ united John with Mary, uniting the purified soul principle with the life-bestowing principle, for further activity on earth:

> At the foot of the cross stood his mother with Lazarus-John, the disciple "whom the Lord loved" and whom he himself had initiated. Through John, the wisdom of Christianity was to flow into posterity; his influence on human astral bodies would allow them to be indwelt by the Christ-Principle. The Christ-Principle was to live there in the human astral body, and it would stream in through John. To this end, however, the Christ-Principle had to descend from the cross and unite with the etheric principle, that is, with his mother. That is why the Christ calls down from the cross, "From this hour on, this is your mother, and this is your son." This means he is uniting his wisdom with the motherly principle.[134]

Rudolf Steiner tells us that John, through his testimony, his word, and his existence, would enable Christians to purify their soul-bodies, transforming them into organs for Christ's activity. Already in an earlier lecture, Steiner had said:

> Now, however, it was essential for the effect of this [Golgotha] event to be present in real Christians. There had to be something that would allow real Christians to begin to develop purified astral bodies (in the Christian sense). Something had to enable them to gradually transform their astral bodies to resemble a "Virgin Sophia" and thus to receive the "Holy Spirit," which could otherwise spread out over the earth but could be received only by individuals with such astral bodies. There had to be something with the power to transform the human astral body into a "Virgin Sophia."
>
> And where does that power lie? It lies in the fact that Christ Jesus had entrusted the disciple whom he loved (that is, the enlightened author of the John Gospel) with the mission of truly and faithfully recording these events in Palestine, so they could affect people. When people allow the contents of the John Gospel to work on them sufficiently, their astral bodies are on the way to becoming a "Virgin Sophia" and receptive to the "Holy Spirit." Through the force of impulses emanating from the John Gospel, the astral body gradually becomes receptive, first sensing and later discerning true spirit. This is the mission or task Christ Jesus assigned to the author of the John Gospel. If you simply read the Gospel, you will find it written there, "By the cross stood Jesus' mother"—the Virgin Sophia of esoteric Christianity—and from the cross the Christ speaks to the disciple whom he loved, saying, "From now on, this is your mother. And from that moment the disciple took her into his home" (John 19:27). In other words, Christ is saying, "I am conveying to you the power

that was in my astral body and enabled it to become a vehicle of the Holy Spirit; you are to write down what this astral body was able to achieve through its development." "And the disciple took her into his home" means that he wrote the John Gospel. In that Gospel, the author has concealed the forces for developing the "Virgin Sophia." At the Crucifixion, he is given the mission of taking her as his mother, of being the Messiah's true and legitimate interpreter.[135]

Rudolf Frieling also wrote:

After speaking words for his enemies [*"Father, forgive them; they do not know what they are doing"* (Luke 23:34)]; and for the enemy who became a friend [*"I tell you this: today you shall be with me in Paradise"* (Luke 23:43)]; Christ turns to those who have always been his friends and have now found the courage and strength to stand at the foot of the cross. *"Mother, there is your son"*; and *"There is your mother."* (John 19:26) Dying, he establishes a new, deeper community between his mother and the disciple he loves, and from that moment John "took her into his own." The Greek, "his own," *ta idia*, is a phrase familiar to us from the beginning of the John Gospel: "He entered his own realm, and his own would not receive him." (John 1:11) This phrase denotes the realm of the "I," of the consciousness of being an individual. It resounds again in the farewell discourses. "You will be scattered, each to his own, and leave me alone" (John 16:32). On Good Friday, it resounds for the third time, but this time it does not mean being encapsulated in selfhood and isolation. It means the "own being," the independent existence that, when imbued by the Christ Being, can open up, making true, profound community possible for the first time."

Esoteric Christian cognition saw Mary, "pierced to the

heart" (Luke 2:35) by the sword of the most profound suffering, as especially related to "Sophia," divine wisdom. At Jesus' conception, she is illumined by the Holy Spirit; at Pentecost, in the midst of the circle of apostles, she experiences the descent of the Holy Spirit. The pain the *mater dolorosa* suffered prepared her soul to be imbued with the "wisdom from above"; "realms of suffering" are transformed into "realms of radiance." Christ unites the disciple with her in the ultimate "own," the "I"-being who will then write the wisdom-filled John Gospel.[136]

Rudolf Steiner tells us that Christ bequeathed to the disciple whom he loved the "testamentary" task of "proclaiming his true form" in a written testimony, namely, his Gospel.[137] John stays with Christ, the only one to do so of the circle he entered after his initiation. Intimately familiar with (mystic) death, he had a profound understanding of the enactment of the Mystery of Golgotha. He related differently to Christ and to the process of dying than the first disciples did, and was the only member of their community to participate in "what led to the cross" (Rudolf Steiner). While the inner community, the individual disciples, and the Christ's entire esoteric circle failed him, John stayed true to the Lord, his consciousness awake, until the very end. *"Father, into thy hands I commit my spirit"* (Luke 23:46).

*

Emmaus

4.
The Disciples of the Risen One

After his resurrection, Christ engaged his disciples in esoteric instruction and gave them many significant teachings.

— Rudolf Steiner [138]

According to John, Mary Magdalene was the first to encounter the resurrected Christ on Easter Sunday morning, in front of the tomb that she had just found empty:

> Mary stood at the tomb outside, weeping. As she wept, she peered into the tomb; and she saw two angels in white sitting there, one at the head, and one at the feet, where the body of Jesus had lain. They said to her, "Why are you weeping?" She answered, "They have taken my Lord away, and I do not know where they have laid him." With these words she turned round and saw Jesus standing there, but did not recognize him. Jesus said to her, "Why are you weeping? Who is it you are looking for?" Thinking it was the gardener, she said, "If it is you, sir, who removed him, tell me where you have laid him, and I will take him away." Jesus said, "Mary!" She turned to him and said, *"Rabbuni!"* (which is Hebrew for "My Master"). Jesus said, "Do not cling to me, for I have not yet ascended to the Father. But go to my brothers, and tell them that I am now ascending to my Father and your Father, my God and your God." Mary of Magdala went to the disciples with her news. "I have seen the Lord!" she said, and gave them his message. (John 20:11-18)

Within the tomb itself (according to Matthew, Mark, and Luke), an angel had spoken about Christ to the women with Mary Magdalene, saying, "I know you are looking for Jesus who was crucified. He is not here; he has been raised again, as he said he would be. Come and see the place where he was laid, and then go quickly and tell his disciples He has been raised from the dead and is going on before you into Galilee; there you will see him" (Matthew 28:6-7; Mark 16:7). "'Remember what he told you while he was still in Galilee, about the Son of Man: how he must be given up into the power of sinful men and be crucified, and must rise again on the third day.' Then they recalled his words..." (Luke 24:6-7).

John reports that the sight of the empty tomb, the linen wrappings, and the head cloth convinced him and Peter of the reality of the Resurrection. "Until then they had not understood the scriptures, which showed that he must rise from the dead. So the disciples went home again..." (John 20:9-10). At first the community of disciples, who had come together again shortly after fleeing on Good Friday, doubted the women's report. "But the story appeared to them to be nonsense, and they would not believe them" (Luke 24:11). "But when they were told that he was alive and that she had seen him, they did not believe it" (Mark 16:11).

*

In the late afternoon on Easter Sunday, two of the disciples were walking toward Emmaus, a village near Jerusalem, "talking together about all these happenings" (Luke 24:14). As the disciples were weighing the events of the last few days in their hearts and struggling to gain an initial understanding, "Jesus himself came up and walked along with them; but something kept them from seeing who it was" (Luke 24:15-16). "The two men are so deep in conversation that they scarcely notice the arrival of a third. So he walked along with them, listening in silence."[139] But then Christ spoke to them, and they stopped walking. "He asked them, 'What is it you are debating as you walk?'" (Luke 24:16). As they continued on their way, they talked about everything that had happened with their teacher, who "appeared as a prophet" and was then condemned and crucified. They told of their grief and disappointment: "We had been hoping that he was the man to liberate Israel" (Luke 24:21). And they told of what happened that morning in the tomb: "And now some women of our company have astounded us; they went early to the tomb, but failed to find his body, and returned with a story that they had seen a vision of angels who told them he was alive. So some of our people went to the tomb and found things just as the women had said, but him they did not see" (Luke 24:22-24).

Thereupon Christ instructed them again about the Messiah's destiny, explaining the Holy Scripture just as he had done in years past. "Then he began with Moses and all the prophets, and explained to them the passages which referred to himself in every part of the scriptures," up to and including the suffering Christ was destined to experience on Golgotha as a prerequisite to his glorification. *"Was the Messiah not bound to suffer thus before entering upon his glory?"* (Luke 24:27-26).

Only when they had arrived in Emmaus, entered the house, and sat down to a shared meal did they recognize the Lord as he blessed, broke, and distributed the bread. "Then their eyes were opened, and they recognized him." Immediately, however, the figure of the Resurrected One withdrew from them again. "He vanished from their sight" (Luke 24:32). Mark's Gospel also mentions these two disciples' encounter with the risen Christ. "Later he appeared in a different guise to two of them as they were walking, on their way into the country" (Mark 16:12).

Luke and Mark both report that the two disciples immediately returned to the community of disciples in Jerusalem after this experience in Emmaus:

> There they found that the Eleven and the rest of the company had assembled, and were saying, "It is true: the Lord has risen; he has appeared to Simon." Then they gave their account of the events of their journey and told how he had been recognized by them at the breaking of the bread.
> As they were talking about all this, there he was, standing among them. And he said to them, "Peace be with you!" Startled and terrified, they thought they were seeing a

ghost. But he said, "Why are you so perturbed? Why do questionings arise in your minds? Look at my hands and feet. It is I myself. Touch me and see; no ghost has flesh and bones as you can see that I have." After saying this he showed them his hands and feet. They were still unconvinced, still wondering, for it seemed too good to be true. So he asked them, "Have you anything here to eat?" They offered him a piece of fish they had cooked and a honeycomb, which he took and ate before their eyes.

And he said to them, "This is what I mean by saying, while I was still with you, that everything written about me in the Law of Moses and in the prophets and psalms was bound to be fulfilled." Then he opened their minds to understand the scriptures. "This," he said, "is what is written: that the Messiah is to suffer death and to rise from the dead on the third day, and that in his name repentance bringing the forgiveness of sins is to be proclaimed to all nations. Begin from Jerusalem; it is you who are the witnesses to it all. And mark this: I am sending upon you my Father's promised gift; so stay here in this city until you are armed with the power from above" (Luke 24:33-49).

In Mark's account, the apostolic community also doubted the two members' report of events in Emmaus: "But again no one believed them" (Mark 16:13). Then, however, "as they were still talking," the Risen One appeared in their midst. "Afterward while the Eleven were at table he appeared to them and reproached them for their incredulity and dullness, because they had not believed those who had seen him after he was raised from the dead" (Mark 16:14).

Christ appears "in the midst" of his circle of disciples, in accordance with his words during the Last Supper, "Yet here I am among you like a servant" (Luke 22:27): and with the true words spoken earlier by John the Baptist. "Among you, though you do not know him, stands the one…" (John 1:26). As yet, no true knowledge of the Christ Being and the Mystery of Golgotha exists within the community of disciples, the "learners in the kingdom of Heaven" (Matthew 13:52). Nonetheless, the disciples were deeply moved by these experiences. Christ, the Risen One, appeared to them, blessing them with words of peace ("Peace be with you!"), a blessing he repeated that Easter Sunday evening, when he made the Holy Spirit accessible to the disciples for the first time, foreshadowing Pentecost. "Jesus repeated, 'Peace be with you!', and said, 'As the Father sent me, so I send you'. Then he breathed on them, saying, 'Receive the Holy Spirit! If you forgive any man's sins, they stand forgiven; if you pronounce them unforgiven, unforgiven they remain'" (John 20:21-23).

*

One week later, on the following Sunday, Christ appeared again "in the midst" of the community of disciples:

> One of the Twelve, Thomas, that is "the Twin," had not been with the rest when Jesus came [on Easter Sunday evening]. So the disciples told him, "We have seen the Lord." He said, "Unless I see the mark of the nails on his hands, unless I put my finger into the place where the nails were, and my hand into his side, I will not believe it."
> A week later the disciples were again in the room, and Thomas was with them. Although the doors were locked, Jesus came and stood among them, saying, "Peace be with you!" Then he said to Thomas, "Reach your finger here; see my hands. Reach your hand here and put it into my side. Be unbelieving no longer, but believe." Thomas said, "My Lord and my God!" Jesus said, "Because you have seen me you have found faith. Happy are they who never saw me and yet have found faith."

When Thomas says, *"My Lord and my God,"*

He has a direct perception of the reality and divine majesty of the Risen One. In accounts of the events of Easter, The words of adoration and recognition from Thomas shine out like the sun. Modern religious historical research indicates that the phrase "Lord and God" is used especially in reference to the Sun-God. One week after Mary Magdalene's direct, personal, soul-borne call, *"Rabbuni!"* ("my master"), The words of Thomas complete it with the reference to sun-like spirit. In addition to the "master," the glorified person of Jesus, these words acknowledge not only the *kyrios* (Lord) in his sun-glory but above him "God," the eternal logos which the prologue of this same Gospel calls "a god." These words spoken by Thomas signify that the Easter Sun has fully risen into the disciples' consciousness.[140]

Nonetheless, in the days and weeks that followed, the disciples struggled repeatedly to experience the Christ in each encounter with the Risen One. John describes how he himself was the only one to recognize the Lord at their meeting at the Sea of Tiberias. "The disciples did not know that it was Jesus" (John 21:4). Although this group of disciples also included Peter, James, and John the son of Zebedee (the witnesses on Mount Tabor), only the disciple "whom Jesus loved" recognized the figure on the shore as the Risen One. "It is the Lord!" (John 21:7); *ho kyrios estin*, which also means "the Lord *is*."[141]

*

Rudolf Steiner said that the disciples "witnessed the Resurrection" (Acts 1:22) through "eyes that became clairvoyant" as a result of the Mystery of Golgotha.[142] In connection with various encounters between the disciples and the Risen

One, Steiner spoke of "The Christ Being's effects on the unconscious" of individual disciples' souls, saying:

> As the Christ worked from being to being after the so-called resurrection, knowledge of the Son rose from the disciples' unconscious soul forces into their soul activity. This accounts for the differences in their descriptions of the risen Christ and for the different ways in which the Christ worked on or appeared to one or the other of them, in accordance with each one's nature. As such, the Christ Being's effects on his disciples' subconscious souls are highly individual, so we must not be put off by the fact that these phenomena are not described consistently but in a great variety of ways.[143]

For the disciples, their encounters with the Risen One were immeasurably important, convincing them of the spiritual reality of the Resurrection. "We can therefore say that for forty days in a row, it was clear to the disciples that Christ was still there."[144] "That he *was there*—that was proof for the disciples. And if we had asked these disciples about the actual content of their faith as they gradually became convinced that the Christ still lived, although he had died, they would have said, "We have proof that Christ lives!" But they would not have spoken at all the way Paul spoke in describing his experience of the event at Damascus."[145]

As Rudolf Steiner also emphasized:

> Paul does not say that the other apostles saw Christ in the physical body, for if he did he would also have to claim that he himself saw Christ in the physical body. He specifically states that he saw Christ in the clouds—that is, the suprasensory Christ—and when he says that he and the other apostles saw Christ, he is indicating that they, like him, saw Christ in his suprasensory body. Of course people

object that Thomas the doubter had to put his hands into Christ's wounds, but that simply means the experience of Christ's presence was so strong that even Thomas was firmly convinced that he touched him. All of these incidents, therefore, referred to the suprasensory Christ.

Of course all of Christ's followers, and the apostles in particular, took Christ's wounds deeply to heart. The Gospel descriptions would be much less vivid if they did not include touching the wounds. But why specifically the wounds? Why does Thomas not lay his hands on Christ's face or the like? He would have been just as able to sense his presence. But he laid his fingers on the wounds because those wounds had made a unique impression, and what the disciples actually perceived of the Christ in this instance depended on higher vision.[146]

Rudolf Steiner tells us that the "suprasensory Christ," the risen Christ "in his suprasensory body," was of central and crucial importance to the disciples. Beginning on Easter Sunday morning, they had spiritual experiences in bodily form; that is, they experienced Christ's etheric spirit-body. The suprasensory character of these modes of experience was always obvious; the Risen One vanished as soon as the disciples recognized him at Emmaus; he appeared "in the midst" of the circle of disciples although the doors were locked. "The Body which appeared before them was not palpable to earthly senses."[147] Even in the three preceding years, says Rudolf Steiner, the Christ had sometimes been present in ways that transcended physical existence. Now, with the Resurrection complete, the disciples saw the Lord in the transformed, transfigured sphere of his being's formative forces. They saw his "ether body condensed to the point of physical visibility:"[148]

> The events that took place during the Christ's sojourn in the body of Jesus of Nazareth lead ultimately to the actual,

physical death of that body. The spirit of Christ spent three days outside of the physical body but then returned, not to the physical body but to the ether body, which had become so dense that the disciples were able to perceive it, as described in the Gospels, allowing Christ to walk among them and become visible even after the event of Golgotha.[149]

What the disciples saw was not his physical body but his ether body, his suprasensory body. The women and the disciples saw Christ in his ether body; no longer as Jesus of Nazareth, but as a transformed inner human being.[150]

Emil Bock writes, "When Thomas sought to touch His hands and His side, the faculties of perception in his own etheric body were so highly enhanced by entering into relation with the life-body of Christ that the powerful tendency of this Body to take on form and substance revealed itself to him as something verging on the physical."[151] The disciples' experiences with the Risen One in the forty days leading up to his Ascension are definitely related to Paul's later experience, with which they share an *etheric* dimension. "Paul's experiences with the Risen One were no different from those of the disciples."[152]

Immediately after the event of Golgotha, however, the inner community of disciples clearly did not have access to Paul's spiritual maturity and certainty. The disciples were full of sorrow, unrest, despair, and longing. Their ability to "behold" arose out of such forces and out of their intense inner connection to Christ. In a lecture to theologians, Rudolf Steiner said:

> Of course you must imagine what happened there as an extraordinarily powerful experience for the disciples. Just imagine your emotional state if you had grown very close to someone who was then taken away from you through crucifixion (or the modern equivalent). That emotional state gave the disciples the clairvoyant ability to perceive

such things. In those first few days, they really did see the Christ, and even more often than the Gospels mention. But it was the suprasensory Christ they saw.[153]

Both individually and in common, the disciples "saw" the suprasensory Christ *"through the strength of their connection to the Christ."*[154] On the basis of this connection, which transcended their consciousness and persisted on deeper soul levels, they were able to perceive him repeatedly.

*

In Acts 1:3, Luke writes, "He showed himself to [the disciples] after his death, and gave ample proof that he was alive; over a period of forty days he appeared to them and taught them about the kingdom of God." According to Luke, Christ not only appeared to the disciples, but also spoke with them, teaching them about the "kingdom of God." "During the forty days between his Resurrection and his Ascension, He is said to have imparted to his disciples the most intimate secrets of the spiritual life and the Word of the Spirit."[155]

Rudolf Steiner spoke on various occasions about the "teachings of the Risen One" given to "individual selected pupils."[156] "Christ engaged his disciples in esoteric instruction and gave them many significant teachings."[157] Steiner tells us that the most important teachings humanity received came "not from the Christ who lived in a physical body until the Mystery of Golgotha, but rather from the risen Christ, after the Mystery of Golgotha."[158] Rudolf Steiner mentioned early Gnostic knowledge of these facts, specifically referring to the Coptic document *Pistis Sophia* (possibly authored by Basilius Valentinus) and a few surviving fragments of other Gnostic literature.[159] Emil Bock writes, "[Gnostic literature] was concerned with the secret of the Forty Days. It is a great loss to the spiritual history of humankind that this literature has fallen victim to the persecutions which were directed by the Church against the Gnostic influence."[160] But as Steiner emphasized, "Spiritual science or spiritual cognition can ascertain what the Christ said after his death to those closest to him, when he appeared to them in his spiritual nature."[161] "Today, anything beyond the sparse information the Gospels provide about the Christ after the Mystery of Golgotha must be rediscovered through anthroposophical spiritual science. We must rediscover what the risen Christ said. What did he say to other disciples not mentioned in the Gospels? The disciples who the Gospels name as encountering Christ Jesus on the road to Emmaus or in the context of the group of apostles all belong to a tradition of very simple souls who cannot advance to esoteric levels. Thus we must go beyond these accounts and ask, what did the Christ say after his Resurrection to his truly initiated pupils?"[162]

In The Hague on Maundy Thursday, 1922, Rudolf Steiner said:

> I can attempt to clothe it only in weak, stammering words because our languages offer nothing better. The human body has gradually become so dense and the death forces in it so strong, that although human beings can develop intellect and freedom, they do so only in a life in which death makes an obvious incision; and any view of the eternal soul is extinguished during waking consciousness. "Your souls, however," said the Christ, the divine teacher, to his initiated pupils, "can receive the specific knowledge that what happened in my own being through the Mystery of Golgotha can also fill you if you simply rise to the insight that Christ has descended from supraearthly spheres to earthly human beings; and that therefore something now exists on earth that cannot be perceived by earthly means, but only through higher means. You will be able to receive this wisdom if you can behold the Mystery of Golgotha as the insertion of a divine event into earthly life; if you can

perceive that a divinity endured the Mystery of Golgotha. Through all other earthly events, you can acquire earthly wisdom, but it is of no use to you in understanding death as it applies to humans (or at least it would be of use only if you, like the people of earlier times, were less intensely interested in death. But because you must be interested in death, your insight depends on a power that is stronger than any earthly power of insight, strong enough to realize that the Mystery of Golgotha broke all earthly natural laws. If your faith is based only on earthly natural law, you will be able to see death, but you will never grasp its significance for human life. If, however, you can rise to the insight that earthly existence receives meaning only at the midpoint of the Earth stage of evolution, through the divine event of the Mystery of Golgotha that cannot be understood by earthly means, then you are cultivating the power of *Pistis Sophia*, a specific power of wisdom that is the same as the power of faith. You invoke a powerful force in your soul when you say, 'I believe (or I know through faith) what I can never believe or know through earthly means. This knowing depends on a stronger force than anything I can claim to know through exclusively earthly means.' In spite of all earthly science, human beings remain weak if their wisdom is capable of grasping only what can be grasped by earthly means. Those who would acknowledge the activity of supraearthly forces in earthly matters must develop much greater inner activity."[163]

The "teachings of the Risen One" pertained to the "mysteries of birth and death" in view of events on Golgotha, and of Christ's earthly experiences on his journey toward undergoing and overcoming death—"very specific mysteries," as Rudolf Steiner called them.[164] Steiner said that Christ experienced "the actual Earth-mystery" through Golgotha. As a divine being, he had decided of his own free will to undergo earthly death in order to save humanity from Ahriman's might.[165] The fact that he overcame death formed a significant part of his teachings on behalf of humanity after the Resurrection. "The lesson Christ imparted to his intimate disciples after the Resurrection was the most fundamental revelation in earthly life, the spiritual foundation of the continued life of the human soul."[166]

The teachings of the Risen One had to do with the human soul and the history of humanity; with the cosmic struggle between the hierarchies and Ahriman; and with the cosmic essence of the Resurrection and Christ's resurrection-body.[167] These teachings also encompassed the inner content of the three sayings or formulas that would later be taught in Rosicrucian schools of esoteric Christianity: *ex Deo nascimur; in Christo morimur; per Spiritum Sanctum reviviscimus*. Rudolf Steiner tells us that as Christ walked among his disciples in spirit form, he spoke to them about existence before birth and after death, about the mystery of human incarnation and excarnation:

> He spoke to them as the great healer, as the therapist and comforter aware of the secret that human beings had formerly been able to recall him because they had been together with him in suprasensory worlds in pre-earthly existence. And now he could say to them, "I once gave you the capacity to recall your suprasensory, pre-earthly existence. And now, if you receive me into your hearts and souls, I will give you the strength to pass through death's portal conscious of your immortality. You will no longer recognize only the Father (*ex deo nascimur*); you will also sense the Son as the one in whom you can die, and yet live (*in Christo morimur*).
>
> Of course all this was not couched in the words I speak now, but this is the meaning of the teachings Christ imparted to those who were close to him after his bodily death. In primeval times, human beings did not know death. From the time when they first achieved consciousness, they were

inwardly aware of the soul element in them that cannot die. They were able to see people around them die, but dying was merely an illusion in the realities that surrounded them. They did not sense death as a reality. By the time the Mystery of Golgotha was approaching, however, human souls had gradually become so body-bound that people began to sense death as a reality; that is, to question whether the soul can continue to live when the body succumbs. That doubt would have been nonexistent in earlier times when people knew about the soul.

And then the Christ appeared as the one who said, "I will live with you on earth so you will have the strength to enkindle in your souls the inner impulse that will allow you to be carried through death as living souls."[168]

In Dornach on June 4, 1924, shortly before the last Whitsun of his life, Rudolf Steiner spoke again about the cosmic aspects of the Risen One's circumstances and teachings. The disciples had early been aware of the Christ Being's spiritual connection to the sun. Rudolf Steiner said that they sensed and acknowledged this connection "instinctively" during the three years:

> We can look into the minds of the disciples and apostles, who knew instinctively that the being who had formerly dwelt exclusively in the sun had descended to earth and now walked among them as Christ Jesus. They also realized that sunlight shone upon them out of the eyes of Jesus of Nazareth and that the sun's warming strength spoke to them out of his words. When Jesus of Nazareth walked among them, it was as if the sun itself was sending its light and strength out into the world. Those who recognized him were aware that previously, the Sun-Being who now walked among them in human form had been accessible only when people lifted their gaze toward the spiritual world itself. Realizing this, the disciples and apostles

were also able to understand and relate to Christ's death in the right way. That is why they were able to remain his disciples even after Christ Jesus had undergone death on earth.[169]

After the Resurrection, Christ Jesus taught the disciples about far-reaching cosmic connections related to the mystery of human life (and death):

> To his intimate disciples, Christ said, Look at life on earth. It is related to the life of the cosmos. When you behold the earth and the surrounding cosmos, it is the Father who imbues them with life. The Father God is the god of space. I, however, am to proclaim to you that I have come from the sun, from time, from the time in which human beings become embedded only when they die. I have come to you from out of time. If you receive me (so said Christ), you receive time and do not succumb to space. But you must also find the transition from the earthly trinity (existence in the physical, etheric, and astral realms) to the other, cosmic trinity (existence in the etheric, astral, and spirit-self). Just as the physical, earthly element cannot be found in the cosmos, spirit-selfhood is not present in earthly reality. But I bring you news of it because I come from the sun.
> Yes, the sun has a threefold aspect. When we are living in the sun and look away from it toward the earth, we see physical, etheric, and astral existence; but if we observe what is present in the sun itself, we constantly see spirit-selfhood. We see physical nature when we look at or remember the earth, but when we look away from it, we see spirit-selfhood on the other side. We alternate between physical existence and spirit-selfhood; between them, only the etheric and astral elements remain stable. When we look out into the cosmos, the earthly element vanishes entirely; what exists there is etheric, astral, and spirit-self.

That is what will come into view when you enter the suntime between death and a new birth.

Imagine it like this. When human beings' soul constitution is fully encapsulated in earthly being, they can sense the divine element because they have been born out of it: *ex Deo nascimur*.

Then let us suppose that instead of being merely encapsulated in the spatial world, we receive the Christ who has come from the temporal world into the spatial world, bringing time itself into earthly space. In death, therefore, he overcomes death. *Ex Deo nascimur; In Christo morimur*.

The Christ, however, brings the good news. When space has been overcome and the sun acknowledged as the creator of space, when we feel ourselves transported through Christ into the living sun, then the physical, earthly element disappears, and the etheric and astral aspects remain. The etheric aspect comes alive; now not as the blue of the heavens, but as the pale red glow of the cosmos, from which the stars no longer merely shine down, but touch us with their loving effects. If we really become aware of these effects as we stand on earth, we feel that the physical aspect is stripped away but the etheric remains, raying into and through us in pale red, while the stars are no longer gleaming points of light but radiant love, like a loving human caress. We sense the divine in us, the divine cosmic fire flaming up out of human nature. We feel ourselves in the etheric cosmos, experiencing manifestations of spirit in the astral radiance of the cosmos. All this elicits in us an inner experience of the spirit radiance to which we are called in the cosmos.

When those who received this proclamation from the Christ had sufficiently imbued themselves with its content, they experienced its effects in the fiery tongues of Pentecost. As the earth's physical aspect fell away, they did sense death, but they also sensed: This is not death; in place of the physical earth, the spirit-selfhood of the universe dawns. *Per Spiritum Sanctum revivisciumus*.[170]

*

Rudolf Steiner tells us that this is how the risen Christ taught his disciples, and that he also gave them other prayers, as the *Pistis Sophia* attests. For the first and only time, in a lecture in Dornach on January 2, 1916, Steiner disclosed one of the prayers Christ communicated to the disciples after Golgotha, a prayer for the human soul in its struggle with the adversarial forces. "O ye powers in the spiritual world, allow me to leave my physical body for the world of light, to exist knowingly in the light." Steiner went on to say, "During that time, these intimate disciples of Christ Jesus learned what I have indicated to you here. They knew about everything we have talked about here today. They knew all about it; they learned it during the time Christ spent with them after the Mystery of Golgotha."[171]

The disciples "knew all about it," but only on deeper soul levels beyond reach of their day-consciousness. "When they were together and discussing among themselves, Christ Jesus was also present among them in his etheric body, *without their knowing it*; and talked with them and they with him; *but for them all this took place as if in a dream, as if they were sleep-walking.*"[172]

*

The Ascension of Christ

5.
Ascension and Pentecost

He who has faith in me will do what I am doing;
and he will do greater things still because
I am going to the Father.
— John 14:14

I̲n̲ ̲h̲i̲s̲ ̲A̲c̲t̲s̲ ̲o̲f̲ ̲t̲h̲e̲ ̲A̲p̲o̲s̲t̲l̲e̲s̲, Luke writes about the end of the forty days:

> While he was in their company he told them not to leave Jerusalem. "You must wait," he said, "for the promise made by my Father, about which you have heard me speak: John, as you know, baptized with water, but you will be baptized with the Holy Spirit, and within the next few days."
>
> So, when they were all together, they asked him, "Lord, is this the time when you are to establish once again the sovereignty of Israel?" He answered, "It is not for you to know about dates or times, which the Father has set within his own control. But you will receive power when the Holy Spirit comes upon you; and you will bear witness for me in Jerusalem, and all over Judaea and Samaria, and away to the ends of the earth."
>
> When he had said this, as they watched, he was lifted up, and a cloud removed him from their sight. As he was going, and as they were gazing intently into the sky, all at once there stood beside them two men in white who said, "Men of Galilee, why stand there looking up into the sky? This Jesus, who has been taken away from you to heaven, will come in the same way as you have seen him go."
>
> Then they returned to Jerusalem from the hill called Olivet, which is near Jerusalem, no farther than a Sabbath day's journey. Entering the city they went to the room upstairs where they were lodging: Peter and John and James and Andrew, Philip and Thomas, Bartholomew, and Matthew, James the son of Alphaeus, and Simon the Zealot, and Judas the son of James. All these were constantly at prayer together, and with them a group

of women, including Mary the mother of Jesus, and his brothers. (Acts 1:4-14)

After the forty days of his spiritual journey with the disciples, after all his "discourses" and "teachings," the Risen One was "taken up" (Acts 1:2 and 11), "carried up" (Luke 24:51), or "lifted up" (Acts 1:9). "Christ's way of still being visible to the apostles and disciples after his resurrection ended with his Ascension."[173] The Risen One rose beyond the disciples' ability to perceive him. Rudolf Frieling writes, "[The Christ] does not cease to bless the disciples with his loving attention; they simply cease to perceive it as the Risen One is glorified, entering a more exalted, more spiritualized mode of existence. At that point, the disciples' ability to perceive him reaches its limits. They are no longer able to follow; their consciousness cannot keep pace with the grandeur of events. He 'outgrows' their capacity for suprasensory perception, as is expressed in the image of him rising out of their sight."[174]

Christ was not really "going away" from the disciples he left behind. "Christ remains fully devoted to his own—devoted as only he can be. He spreads his arms out over them and blesses them, meaning that he allows his being to flow into them; he is totally there for them."[175]

At the conclusion of his Gospel, Luke describes the Ascension. "Then he led them out as far as Bethany, and blessed them with uplifted hands; and in the act of blessing he parted from them" (Luke 24:50-51). Or, as Rudolf Frieling translates: "And it happened that *while he was blessing them*, he parted from them and was carried up into heaven."[176]

Immediately before this blessing, Christ had again spoken to the disciples about the imminent arrival of the Holy Spirit, which he had also proclaimed on Maundy Thursday. "But you will receive power when the Holy Spirit comes upon you." The disciples would then bear witness to the Christ Event far beyond Palestine. "And you will bear witness for me in Jerusalem, and all over Judaea and Samaria, and away to the ends of the earth" (Acts 1:8). "*Earth* is the Risen One's last word as he disappears. His view and his will are directed toward the whole earth."[177] According to Matthew's account, the risen Christ promised the disciples his renewed support for the future. "And be assured, I am with you always, to the end of time" (Matthew 28:20).

"As on Easter Sunday morning at the empty grave, two angels again appeared, flanking the disciples' newly empty field of vision."[178] "As he was going, and as they were gazing intently into the sky, all at once there stood beside them two men in white" (Acts 1:10). Whereas the angels by the tomb had questioned Mary Magdalene's sorrowful weeping at the absence of the corpse, the angels on the Mount of Olives questioned the disciples' fruitless efforts to see the Lord, who was no longer perceptible to them. "Men of Galilee, why stand there looking up into the sky?" (Acts 1:11) Then the angels proclaimed Christ's imminent return and the beginning of a new vision after dramatic events to follow, as Christ himself had done in the same place. "This Jesus, who has been taken away from you up to heaven, will come in the same way as you have seen him go" (Acts 1:11).

Deeply moved, the disciples returned in silence to the Upper Room in Jerusalem. "All these were constantly at prayer together, and with them a group of women, including Mary the mother of Jesus, and his brothers." (Acts 1:14)

*

Rudolf Frieling, writing about the Ascension as the "conclusion and crowning of the process the resurrection body underwent during the forty days," and about the Christ Being's assimilation into the spiritual world, says:

> The human nature the Christ had assumed and then transformed through his death and resurrection is received by the higher worlds. Humanity, as sanctified by the Christ,

is "incorporated" into the heavens as a new, enriching element on the levels of spirit, soul, and even body. In the Luke Gospel, the words "taken up" summarize the entire Mystery of Golgotha, from death through resurrection to ascension. "As the time approached when he was to be taken up to heaven, he set his face resolutely toward Jerusalem." (Luke 9:51)[179]

Rudolf Steiner also spoke about Christ's transformation (or, as Frieling calls it, sanctification) of humanity in connection with the Ascension. Steiner said that the Mystery of Golgotha— the Christ's passage through earthly death—took place at a critical juncture in humanity's evolution. In the times leading up to this event, the descending evolutionary processes of the earth organism had also taken hold of the human physical body, resulting in the real danger that in future, human incarnation would be blocked. The Mystery of Golgotha counteracted that possibility. "In fact, by the time the Mystery of Golgotha was enacted, the collaboration of Ahrimanic and Luciferic powers had brought humanity almost to the point of dying off on earth. Through the Mystery of Golgotha, humanity was healed and saved from extinction."[180] Rudolf Steiner said that the Christ's decisive act of turning toward the earth in the Mystery of Golgotha was an objective cosmic event that resulted in a seminal vitalization of the human physical body, a "rekindling" of the "physical human being's forces of growth and health."[181] After forty days of instruction in the mysteries of the Earth stage of evolution, the disciples perceived this process at the Ascension, although (at least partially) from the opposite perspective. "They confronted, in concrete spiritual form, what would have happened if the event of Golgotha had not taken place."[182] The disciples saw not only how etheric forces were attempting to return to their origins in the cosmic sphere of the sun, but also how the Christ gathered up these life forces and reconnected them to the earth:

To the soul eyes of his disciples, Christ was ascending. This means that their soul eyes were magically shown how the upward-striving human etheric element unites with the power and impulse of the Christ. At the time of the Mystery of Golgotha, the human ether body was in danger of being drawn up into the clouds, toward the sun. The Christ, however, held together what was streaming sunward.

To understand this image correctly, we must see it as a warning. Although Christ remains united with the earth, he actually belongs to the sunward-striving forces in the human being that are attempting to escape from the earth for all time to come. The Christ-Impulse, however, holds human beings firmly on earth.

Thus this image of the Ascension revealed to the disciples' soul eyes what would have come to pass if the Mystery of Golgotha had not occurred.[183]

The disciples, having become clairvoyant, see the sunward-striving tendency of human etheric bodies. Christ unites with this striving and restrains it. This, then, is the mighty image of Ascension: the salvation of the human physical/etheric element through the Christ.[184]

Through the Mystery of Golgotha, Christ preserved the "sunward-striving etheric" element for the earth. He united with its future development, with the forces that shape life in the human being. *"This sunward-striving element restrained by the Christ reveals the fact that the Christ remains united with humanity on earth."*[185]

*

"Then they returned to Jerusalem from the hill called Olivet, which is near Jerusalem, no farther than a Sabbath day's journey. Entering the city they went to the room upstairs where they were lodging: Peter and John and James and Andrew, Philip and Thomas, Bartholomew and Mathew, James the son of Alphaeus, and Simon the Zealot, and Judas the son of James. All these were constantly at prayer together, and with them a group of women, including Mary the mother of Jesus, and his brothers." (Acts 1:12-14)

Quietly and solemnly, the disciples returned from the Mount of Olives after the Ascension and retreated into their inner space. Rudolf Steiner said that a growing sorrow came over them. They had been moved by their vision and experienced Christ's blessing as well as his departure. Now, however, he was removed from the realm of their perception. "They saw the figure of the Christ disappear in the clouds—that is, from their consciousness. Of course it seemed to them that the Christ was now no longer on earth, and profound sorrow overcame them."[186] "There came a moment in the life of Christ Jesus' disciples when they realized: We used to see him, but now we do not. He descended from heaven to us here on earth. Where has he gone? The Christian feast of the Ascension commemorates the point when the disciples believed they had once again lost Christ's presence. Once again, the exalted Sun-Spirit who walked the earth in the person of Jesus of Nazareth had disappeared. Having undergone this experience, Christ's disciples were now overcome with a sorrow comparable to none other on earth. In the sun ritual celebrated in the ancient mysteries, the image of the god was laid in the earth to be taken out again after several days, and souls were overcome with great sadness at the death of the god. The extent of this sorrow, however, cannot be compared to the sorrow that now filled the hearts of Christ's disciples."[187]

Rudolf Steiner said, however, that the disciples did not simply spend the entire ten days between Ascension and Pentecost in a passive state of grief. With "inner strength," they reviewed "everything the Christ had ever said to them."[188] "While they were gathered together in the Upper Room, living in the great memories of the last three years, again and again they became aware of certain words and actions of their Master, as fresh and as overwhelming as if they were now being spoken or enacted before them for the first time."[189] Nonetheless, the events of the three years and the Mystery of Golgotha had still not come alive in the disciples' full day-consciousness. Rudolf Steiner described them as "pondering deeply" and "thoughtfully" about where human beings may find the strength to receive the Christ-Impulse into their spirit-soul, now that their physical nature has been saved.[190]

The disciples' great sorrow, however, along with the longing and the unanswered questions they had been left alone to endure, was the prerequisite to the next step in development:

> All real, significant cognition is born out of pain and sorrow. In the ten days after Christ's Ascension, his disciples suffered tremendously because he had vanished from their sight. This pain, this infinite sorrow, then gave rise to what we called the Mystery of Pentecost. After Christ vanished from their superficial instinctive clairvoyance, his disciples found him again within themselves, in what they sensed and experienced through sorrow and pain.[191]
>
> True, profound insight is born out of suffering; and the mystery of Pentecost grew out of the profound soul-suffering Christ's disciples endured after his Ascension. To the disciples' superficial instinctive clairvoyance, Christ disappeared from view, but within them his power came alive. The Christ had sent them the spirit who made it possible for their souls to feel his Christ existence within themselves. This was the content of the first Whitsun festival in humanity's evolution. Whitsun followed the Ascension. At Pentecost, the Christ, who had disappeared from view for the remnants of superficial clairvoyance inherited from ancient times, appeared in the disciples' inner experience. The fiery tongues of Whitsun are nothing other than the Christ coming to life in his disciples' souls. The Whitsun

festival follows on the Ascension as a matter of inner necessity.[192]

Luke writes about the Whitsun event in his Acts of the Apostles:

> While the day of Pentecost was running its course they were all together in one place, when suddenly there came from the sky a noise like that of a strong driving wind, which filled the whole house where they were sitting. And there appeared to them tongues like flames of fire, dispersed among them and resting on each one. And they were all filled with the Holy Spirit and began to talk in other tongues, as the Spirit gave them power of utterance. (Acts 2:1-4)

*

In his farewell discourses, Christ repeatedly proclaimed the mission of the "Holy Spirit" who was to come after his death and resurrection, and he told the disciples that they would achieve insight through this spirit. "And I will ask the Father, and he will give you another to be your Advocate, who will be with you forever—the Spirit of truth. The world cannot receive him, because the world neither sees nor knows him; but you know him, because he dwells with you and is in you" (John 14:16-17). Christ said that the "Spirit of truth" would be with and in the disciples, revealing the Mystery of Christ that they had been able to approach only to a very limited extent during his three earthly years. "However, when he comes who is the Spirit of truth, he will guide you into all the truth; for he will not speak on his own authority, but will tell only what he hears; and he will make known to you the things that are coming. *He will [reveal] me, for everything that he makes known to you he will draw from what is mine.* All that the Father has is mine, and that is why I said, 'Everything he makes known to you he will draw from what is mine'" (John 16:13-15). Christ told the disciples that the "Holy Spirit," the "Spirit of truth," would lead them to consciousness and understanding of the teachings and experiences of his three earthly years. He, the Christ, would send down upon them the "power from above" (Luke 24:49); moreover, he said to them, the "Spirit of truth" "will teach you everything and *call to mind* all that I have told you" (John 14:26).

In a lecture on the Whitsun event, Rudolf Steiner said, "The Christ had sent them the spirit who made it possible for their souls to feel his Christ existence within themselves. This was the content of the first Whitsun festival in humanity's evolution."[193] Elsewhere, Steiner called the awakening of the disciples' memory and consciousness at Whitsun one of the "most significant festivals, and one of the most difficult to understand. ...The festival of Pentecost is related to the deepest mysteries, to humanity's holiest spiritual resources."[194] Rudolf Steiner spoke for the first time about the disciples' awakening and recollecting in Oslo in October 1913, in his lectures on the Fifth Gospel. Here are some excerpts:

> In that moment, the apostles felt as if they were waking up after spending many days in an unaccustomed state of consciousness. It was really somewhat like awakening from deep sleep, albeit a strange, dream-filled sleep that [did not prevent them performing] all of their outer daily tasks. To all appearances, they were functioning as physically healthy people, so others they met did not notice their different state of consciousness. Nonetheless, the moment came when it seemed to the apostles that they had spent days as if in dream-filled sleep from which they awakened during the Whitsun event. They sensed this awakening in a strange way, as if something that could only be called the substance of omnipotent love was descending upon them. As if fructified from above by omnipotent love and as if awakened from their dreamlike state—that was how the apostles felt. They felt as if they were being awakened by the primal power of love that pervades and warms the

cosmos, as if this primal power of love had descended into the soul of each one of them.

To other people observing them and hearing them speak, they seemed quite foreign. These other people knew them as individuals who had formerly lived a very simple life, although recently they had been behaving somewhat strangely, as if lost in dreams. Now, however, they seemed transformed, as if they had undergone a fundamental shift in attitude. They appeared as individuals who had lost all of life's narrowness and selfishness, and gained infinite broad-mindedness; an all-embracing inner tolerance, and a profound and heartfelt understanding of all aspects of human existence on earth. They could also express themselves in ways that anyone present could understand. It was as if they could see into every heart and soul, and know its deepest secrets. As a result, they could comfort anyone, saying exactly what each person needed to hear.

To observers, of course, this sudden transformation in a number of individuals was highly surprising. But how was it for these individuals themselves, who had been awakened by the cosmic spirit of love, so to speak? They now sensed a new inner understanding of events they had not understood when they were happening, even though these events had run their course in close connection with their own souls. Only in this moment, as they felt themselves being fructified with cosmic love, did their soul vision understand what had actually happened on Golgotha.

If we look back with clairvoyant vision into the soul of one apostle in particular (the one usually called Peter in the other Gospels), it is as if his normal earthly consciousness had been completely stripped away, beginning with the moment the other Gospels usually call Peter's denial of the Christ. Now Peter beheld the moment when he was asked if he had any connection to the man from Galilee, and he knew now that he had denied it because his normal consciousness had begun to fade, displaced by an abnormal dream-like state that signified a shift into a very different world. On this first Whitsunday, he felt as if he were waking up in the morning and remembering what had happened just before he had fallen asleep the previous night. That was how Peter recalled events just prior to the onset of that abnormal state; that is, his triple "denial" of the Christ before the cock crowed twice. Then he also remembered that state enveloping his soul just as night envelops a person falling asleep. But Peter also remembered the intervening state as filled, not with mere dream images, but with formations representing a higher state of consciousness in which he witnessed purely spiritual matters. Everything he had "slept through" since that time appeared to his soul as if in a clairvoyant dream. In particular, he now learned to behold the *Mystery of Golgotha*, an event we can truly say he slept through. As it was actually happening, he had not experienced it with understanding, because to understand it fully first required fructification by omnipotent cosmic love, which now allowed images of the Mystery of Golgotha to appear before his eyes.[195]

Among the many images filling Peter's field of consciousness, some stood out: the cross erected on Golgotha, the darkening of the sky at midday, the earthquake. For Peter, these images were the first results of fructification with all-prevailing cosmic love at Whitsun. Now he knew what his normal consciousness had really not known—that the event of Golgotha had taken place, and that the body that hung on the cross was the same body he had often accompanied in life. Now he knew that Jesus had died on the cross; and that this death was actually the birth of the spirit that now, as all-prevailing love, poured into the souls of the apostles gathered for the Whitsun festival. Like a ray of the original, eternal love of the ages, he felt the spirit awakening in his soul as the same spirit that was born when Jesus died on the cross. A tremendous truth descended into Peter's soul: The death on the cross was only an illusion. In reality, that death, preceded by infinite suffering, was the birth of what now streamed into his soul for the sake of the entire earth. For the earth, the death of Jesus signified the birth of the omnipotent cosmic love formerly present everywhere *outside* the earth.

Such words seem easy enough to say in the abstract; but we must really insert ourselves into Peter's soul when he sensed for the first time that as Jesus of Nazareth died on the cross on Golgotha, something was being born on earth that had formerly been present only out in the cosmos. Jesus' death was the birth of all-prevailing cosmic love within the earthly sphere....

This is what the New Testament means by the descent or outpouring of the Holy Spirit. At the time of the death of Jesus of Nazareth, the apostles' soul constitution had not been equipped to participate in the event except in an abnormal state of consciousness.

Peter, John, and James were then forced to recall another moment in their lives, a moment described in the other Gospels but revealed in its full significance only in the Fifth Gospel. The man they had accompanied on earth had led them out to the Mount of Olives, to the garden of Gethsemane, saying, "Stay awake and pray!" But they had fallen asleep; and now they recognized that sleep as the beginning of the state of consciousness that had increasingly enveloped their souls. Their normal consciousness fell into a sleep that lasted throughout the event of Golgotha, and from it radiated what I have haltingly attempted to describe here. Peter, John, and James now recalled falling into this state, and as they looked back, the great events that took place around the body of the One they had accompanied now dawned upon them. Gradually, as if in rapt dreams now appearing to human consciousness, these bygone days appeared in the apostles' consciousness and souls. At the time, they had not experienced all these events with normal consciousness, but now everything they had experienced in their souls' depths during the time from Golgotha to Whitsun descended to the level of ordinary consciousness. They experienced this time (and especially the ten days from Christ's so-called Ascension to Whitsun) as a period of deep sleep. In retrospect, however, their experiences of the days between the Mystery of Golgotha and Christ Jesus' Ascension gradually emerged in a very strange way.... Image after image appeared in the apostles' souls, and these images told them: Yes, you have indeed met the One who died and was born on the cross; you have been in his company.

Sometimes when you wake up in the morning, you remember being together with one or the other person in your dreams. Similarly, memories emerged like dreams in the apostles' souls, but the way these individual events rose to consciousness was unique. The apostles repeatedly had to ask themselves, "Who is this man we were together with?" Again and again, they failed to recognize him. They sensed that it was a spiritual figure; they were certain that they had been in his company in their dreamlike state; but they did not recognize him in the form in which he appeared to them now, when they were fructified with all-prevailing love. They saw themselves in the company of the One we call the Christ, after the Mystery of Golgotha. They also saw how he taught them about the kingdom of spirit. They learned to understand that they had spent forty days with the being who was born on the cross. They saw how this being—the all-prevailing love born out of the cosmos into the earth—had been their teacher, but their normal consciousness had not been ready to understand what he told them, so they had been forced to receive it with their souls' subconscious forces. In Christ's company, they had been like sleepwalkers; their ordinary understanding had been incapable of receiving what that being had to give them. During those forty days, they listened to him with a consciousness they did not recognize, a consciousness that emerged in them only after the Whitsun event. They had listened like sleepwalkers. He had appeared to them as their spiritual teacher and instructed them in mysteries they were able to understand only because he transported them into a very different state of consciousness. Now, for the first time, they realized what had happened to them and recognized the one they had accompanied as the risen Christ. And how were they able to recognize him as the same being they had accompanied in body before the Mystery of Golgotha? It happened like this.

Let's suppose this image appears to the souls of the apostles after the Whitsun festival. They see how they had accompanied and been instructed by the Risen One, whom they had failed to recognize. (They did indeed see a heavenly spiritual being, but they did not recognize who it was.) Then this first image mingles with the purely spiritual image of one of their actual experiences with Christ Jesus prior to the Mystery of Golgotha. First they see Christ Jesus teaching them about the mystery of the spirit, but they do not recognize him. As they hold the image of themselves face-to-face with this spiritual teacher, it gradually transforms into an image of their actual experience of the Last Supper with Christ Jesus. Imagine the apostles' suprasensory experience of the Risen One, together with the image of the Last Supper working in the background. That is how they recognize the One now teaching them (in the very different form he assumed after the Mystery of Golgotha) as the One they once accompanied in body. Recollections emerging from their sleep-like state of consciousness merge completely with earlier recalled images, as if two images were superimposed. One image is of experiences after the Mystery of Golgotha, and another is shining in from a time before their consciousness was so dimmed that they no longer knew what was happening. That is how they recognize the two beings—the Risen One and the one they accompanied in body not long ago—as one and the same. They now realize that before they were awaked through being fructified with all-prevailing cosmic love, they had been removed from their normal state of consciousness while the Christ, the Risen One, was with them. He had taken them, all unknowing, up into his kingdom, revealing its mysteries to them as he accompanied them. Now, after the mystery of Whitsun, these dreamlike experiences were emerging into their normal consciousness.[196]

Rudolf Steiner said that the disciples spent the forty days between the death on Golgotha and the Ascension in the company of Christ, but in a higher state of consciousness. "But Peter also remembered the intervening state as filled, not with mere dream images, but with formations representing a higher state of consciousness in which he witnessed purely spiritual matters."[197] Then the "Holy Spirit" arrived, sent by and associated with the Christ: "What he is to proclaim to you, he takes from my being." Now the disciples really woke up. Finally, after all their searching, their powers of recollection and understanding broke through.[198] "They felt as if they were regaining consciousness in a remarkable way."[199] They were now able to connect their experiences before the Mystery of Golgotha with the events of the forty days, and thus to recognize Christ: "Now they remembered how they had once walked the countryside with the One who was so precious, dear, and important to them. Then, at a certain point, it was as if he was taken away from them. It seemed to them that they were stripped of the memory of accompanying Jesus on the physical plane and experienced subsequent events as if sleepwalking."[200] Rudolf Steiner reported that with their waking Whitsun-consciousness, the disciples first relived the forty days between Golgotha and Ascension: "Now they experienced it in memory." Of Peter's experience and recollection of the Risen One's teachings, Steiner said, "What the Risen One effected in Peter's soul penetrated deeply during the forty days, but became conscious only in retrospect, at Whitsun."[201] Speaking in the context of the Fifth Gospel, Rudolf Steiner described the apostolic community during the forty days. "When they were together among themselves, Christ Jesus was also present in his etheric body. Although they did not know he was there, he spoke with them, and they with him, but they remained as if sleepwalking throughout. The experience became conscious only in retrospect, at Whitsun."[202] *"Now everything we experienced in that other state of consciousness becomes conscious images."*[203]

Then the disciples experienced Golgotha. "They looked back in time and experienced for themselves the resurrection and the death on the cross."[204] In intense images and with spiritually awakened powers of memory and conscience, they experienced the events they had missed, especially the darkening of the sun and the Christ Being's union with the earth *through* that darkness:

> Then we can perceive how, at the death on the cross, the Christ-Impulse passes through this darkness and unites with the earth's aura. In this darkness just before his death, we behold the union of the cosmic Christ-Impulse with the earth's aura. We receive a great, mighty impression of how the Being who had lived in the body of Jesus now pours himself out over the earth's aura of spirit and soul, so that human souls are drawn into it from now on. To spiritually behold the cross on Golgotha in this way, and to see the Christ pouring himself out over earthly life through the darkened earth, is a tremendously overwhelming impression, because what we behold in image form is the actual enactment of an event that was a necessity for earthly humanity's evolution. ...I have just described what the

apostles experienced as the Mystery of Golgotha through looking back on their own encounters with Christ after the resurrection.[205]

Next, the disciples' experience continued back through the three earthly years they spent in the company of Christ Jesus. "Looking backward, and now understanding for the first time, the disciples beheld the three years of Christ Jesus' life from the Baptism by John to the Mystery of Golgotha."[206] In this process, they recapitulated the events immediately preceding Golgotha, when their consciousness was interrupted. Rudolf Steiner said that Peter denied the Christ in a "dreamlike trance."[207] In this altered state of consciousness, which had already begun in Gethsemane and was associated with the disciple's etheric nature, Peter "denies Christ, not due to any moral defect but because it is as if he is sleepwalking. To his ordinary consciousness, his connection with Christ Jesus simply does not exist. When asked, "Are you one of them?" he does not know, because his etheric body has been so transformed that he fails to recognize the connection at that moment."[208]

Rudolf Steiner said that by gaining a comprehensive view of Christ's path, "sensing his existence" within themselves, and at least beginning to understand his deed, the disciples recognized the cosmic-earthly event that took place in the Mystery of Golgotha. In his lectures on the Fifth Gospel, Steiner said:

> At Whitsun, what had taken place for the sake of earth's evolution became clear to them. Something formerly out in the cosmos but now present on earth revealed itself to them. The time from the Baptism to the Mystery of Golgotha is like a gestation period. His death on the cross is birth; the Christ's life with the apostles after his resurrection corresponds to an earthly lifetime; and his transition into the earth's aura corresponds to the human soul's passage into the spiritual world. For the Christ, the process

was the exact opposite. For his own destiny, he sought out the opposite [of the human incarnation process]. Human souls pass from the earth into the spiritual world; the Christ passes from the spiritual world into the sphere of the earth, uniting with the earth and merging into its aura through his great sacrifice. Now, in the earth's aura, the Christ dwells in the devachan he chose for himself. Whereas human beings rise from the earth into heaven, the Christ descends from heaven to the earth to live with human beings. That is his devachan.

In one of the last events of Whitsunday, the image of Christ's Ascension into heaven (actually his journey to earth), of God's entry into his earthly existence, appeared to the spirit vision of the apostles and disciples. They clearly sensed what had happened, what lot had befallen the Earth stage of evolution. At Whitsun, the apostles felt transformed and filled with a new consciousness. *That was the descent of spirit. Spirit-filled cognition lit up within them.*[209]

For the disciples, Steiner said, one of their last insights in the course (or enactment) of the Whitsun festival was the image or cognition that Christ continued to live in the sphere of the earth—as the "soul of the earth."[210] The disciples became able to perceive Christ as a real, lasting presence among human souls on earth. As he had said to them earlier, "I am with you always, even unto the end of the earth."

*

Although the disciples experienced Whitsun together, as a community united by the suffering that preceded this event, the processes of recollection and consciousness made possible by the "[spirit] power from above" (Luke 24:49), the "spirit self-hood" of the cosmos, affected them individually. Peter's remembered experiences of the forty days, Golgotha, and the preceding years were *his alone*, and the same was true of all the other disciples.

As Rudolf Steiner put it in one lecture:

> Fiery tongues descended on each one. Formerly, the individual apostles' souls had felt embedded in the overall aura of the Mystery of Golgotha. Then, during the Whitsun event, what they had once been able to perceive and acknowledge only collectively, as a community, passed over into their individual souls, illuminating them from within.[211]

In this sense, the Whitsun event worked out of individual processes of consciousness and cognition; out of the awakened conscience of the individual; rousing the disciples to "individual spiritual activity"; and allowing them to be "illuminated by its resurrection."[212] As a result, the apostolic community emerged all the stronger, and was able to begin its actual activity on earth.

Luke reports that the disciples began to speak in different languages, to the astonishment of those around them. "And they were all filled with the Holy Spirit and began to talk in other tongues, as the Spirit gave them power of utterance" (Acts2:4). The disciples experienced the event of Whitsun directly and inwardly, as the "feeling and power of their own souls":

> What the disciples were then able to express was convincing even to the Greeks of that time. The inner power of their individual feeling souls, which provided the impetus for what we call Christian evolution, blossomed out of the Fifth Gospel at work in them. They were able to speak as they did, and do what they did, because the Fifth Gospel, which we are now deciphering here, was a living force in their souls; even if they could not express it in words as we must now attempt to do. As if through an act of awakening, they had been fructified by all-prevailing cosmic love, and they continued to be active under the influence of this fructification. What the Christ became after the Mystery of Golgotha was now at work in them.[213]

Rudolf Steiner said that Christ had sent his spirit to the disciples; and that while they maintained and even strengthened their "I"-consciousness, this spirit "allowed their souls to feel his Christ-Existence within themselves. …So the Holy Spirit is actually what the Christ was to send us, so he could indwell human beings while preserving their "I"-consciousness."[214] Now, in a different way than before, the disciples were able to bear witness to him and his *"light of being*…out of the depths of spiritual life," as real "disciples of the Risen One":

> In reality, this means … from that point on they were able to convey the mysteries of Golgotha to every human heart irrespective of its religious beliefs. [215]
>
> Now, however, they appeared transformed, like individuals whose souls had actually acquired entirely new constitutions or fundamental attitudes. It was as if they had lost all of life's narrowness and selfishness and had won infinitely open hearts, an all-embracing inner tolerance, and a profound, heartfelt understanding of being human on earth. Moreover, they could express all this in ways that anyone present could understand. Those around them sensed that the disciples could see into every heart and soul, guess its deepest inner secrets, and console each one by saying exactly the right thing.[216]

Whitsun was the *consummation* of the Mystery of Golgotha, inasmuch as the disciples were now able to bring the Christ-Mystery to human souls; and to create the possibility for those souls to develop a connection to the Christ-Impulse in spirit and soul, in "I" and astral body; now that the objective salvation of human physical nature had been achieved. "In the evolutionary history of humanity, what do the two successive images [of Ascension and Whitsun] tell us? The Ascension image tells us that for the human physical and etheric body, the event of Golgotha took place on the level of all humankind. Individuals must now make it fruitful for themselves by receiving the Holy Spirit, each one for him or herself. This is how the Christ-Impulse becomes individual."[217] The disciples then travelled and taught, witnesses to the Mystery of Golgotha that they had not perceived with physical eyes. Speaking about Peter's Whitsun recollections and subsequent teachings, Rudolf Steiner said:

> With regard to the memory that came to light in a soul such as Peter's, you must think of it as including recollections of events at which that soul was not directly present. Peter, for example, spoke from memory to anyone who would listen to him, teaching them about what he recalled of the Mystery of Golgotha, although he had not been present. This is how the Mystery of Golgotha was taught and revealed.[218]

*

Rudolf Steiner called such souls "disciples of the Risen One."[219] Through the event of Whitsun, through recalling everything they had experienced with and through Christ, they became "apostles" in their "direct faith in the figure of Christ."[220] Or, in Luke's words, *"because my name lives in you"* (Luke 21:12). The disciples became active, teaching and healing, as Christ's farewell discourses foretold:

> He who has faith in me will do what I am doing; and he will do greater things still because I am going to the Father. Indeed, anything you ask in my name I will do, so that the Father may be glorified in the Son. If you ask anything in my name I will do it. (John 14:12-14)

Mark writes, "They went out to make their proclamation everywhere, and *the Lord worked with them* and confirmed their words by the miracles that followed" (Mark 16:20).

In his lectures on the Fifth Gospel, Rudolf Steiner described the dissemination of the "Christian impulse" after Whitsun, in human hearts and in various countries. Many of those who found their way to Christianity embraced the "Christ-Impulse" without any conscious understanding of Christ's being and the Mystery of Golgotha. Rudolf Steiner said that in a certain respect, the Christian impulse spread independently "of human understanding": "Beginning with the event of Whitsun, the stream of Christ's power poured out over the earth."[221] In Kristiania, Steiner explained for the first time in detail that what moved from heart to heart was the *Christ himself*. "We are forced to disregard all of our scientific ideas and point to the reality of the situation, to show how mysteriously Christ himself passed through many thousand impulses; taking shape within souls, descending into thousands and thousands of them, filling human beings down through the centuries. Among the simplest people, it was Christ himself who traversed the Greek and Italian world, taking possession of ever-increasing numbers of human souls to the west and north. Christ himself walked beside the later teachers who brought Christianity to the Germanic peoples. He—the real, veritable Christ—holds sway on earth like the very soul of the earth itself, moving from place to place and from soul to soul, entering these souls regardless of what they think about the Christ."[222] The disciples of the Risen One, however, the community of apostles who awakened at Whitsun, were involved in this process. Having already been imbued with the "spirit of truth," they were ready to take up their "cross" and follow him. "You will bear witness for me in Jerusalem, and all over Judaea and Samaria, and away to the ends of the earth" (Acts 1:8).

> Christendom did not spread out over the world in the apostles' footsteps; rather, in their missionary activities, Christians followed in the footsteps of the Lord.[223]

*

Appendix

The Esoteric (Apostle's) Our Father

According to Rudolf Steiner's spiritual research[224]

Father who was, is, and will be in our inmost being!

Thy being will be glorified and praised in us all.

May thy kingdom expand in our deeds and in our life's journey.

In our life's activity, we perform thy will, just as thou,
O Father, has placed it in our inmost heart and mind.

In the changing circumstances of our life, thou offer us
spirit nourishment, the bread of life, in overabundance.

May our mercy toward others counterbalance sins committed
against our being.

Because no temptation can persist in thy being, thou do not
allow the tempter to work in us through the asset of our
strength; for the tempter is but appearance and illusion, out
of which thou, O Father, will guide us safely by the light
of thy insight.

May thy strength and glory work in us through the course of
all times to come.

The High Priestly Prayer
JOHN 17:1-8, 24, 26

A rendition from the source text by Rudolf Steiner[225]

Jesus, shifting into spirit vision, spoke:
Father-ground of worlds,
Let thy Son's creating be revealed;
That through thy Son's creating
Thou may also be revealed.

Thou has made him the creator
In all fleshly human bodies
That he may live into the future,
Leading all who came to thee through him.

In future they will live
Because their soul's eye is ready
To behold thee as the true and only ground of worlds,
And the creating Christ Jesus
Whom thou hast sent to them.

Through me, thou has been revealed again in earth existence
As the earth enshrouded thy revelation in cloud.
Such was thy will, which worked through me.

So too, Father-ground of worlds,
Let thy revelation now radiate;
The revelation that came into being through me, before thou
Was revealed in the world of earth.

Through me, the word came into being;
The word that reveals thee in human souls
Who came to me through thee;
And they have received into themselves
Knowledge of thee.

By them was recognized
That what thou spoke to them
Was spoken to them
From thee, through me.

Father-ground of worlds, I plead with thee
That those who came to thee through me
May always live with thee
As I am with thee;
And that there they may behold thy revelation,
Which thou lovingly allowed to radiate before me
Before the earth existed.

Through me was revealed the word
That reveals thee;
And I will bear this word into human souls,
That the love with which thou loves me
May be perpetuated in them;
So too may my eternal life
Preserve their life eternally.

Notes

[Translator's note: References from the works of Rudolf Steiner given throughout the following notes refer to the pages of the German editions (GA). Passages have been newly translated to give consistency of terminology.]

1. Rudolf Steiner: *Aus der Akasha-Forschung. Das Fünfte Evangelium.* GA 148. Fifth edition, Dornach 1992, p. 280. In English: *The Fifth Gospel. From the Akashic Record.* Tr. Anna Meuss. Forest Row, U.K.: Rudolf Steiner Press 1998.
2. Ibid. p. 322.
3. Biblical quotations in this English translation are based on the New English Bible, adapted as the sense of Dr. Selg's commentary requires.
4. Rudolf Steiner: *Vorträge und Kurse über christlich-religiöses Wirken, II* [Lectures and courses on Christian religious work, vol. 2]. GA 343. Dornach 1993, p. 297.
5. Friedrich Rittelmeyer: *Briefe über das Johannes-Evangelium.* First edition, Stuttgart 1938, p. 294.
6. Rudolf Steiner: *Vorstufen des Mysteriums von Golgatha.* GA 152, third edition, Dornach 1990, p. 148. In English: *Approaching the Mystery of Golgotha.* Tr. Michael Miller. Great Barrington, MA: SteinerBooks 2006.
7. Rudolf Steiner: *Die menschliche Seele in ihrem Zusammenhang mit göttlich-geistigen Individualitäten.* [The human soul and its connection with divine-spiritual individualities]. GA 224, third edition, Dornach 1992, p. 144.
8. Cf. my analysis of Rudolf Steiner and the Fifth Gospel See *Rudolf Steiner and the Fifth Gospel: Insights into a New Understanding of the Christ Mystery.* Great Barrington, MA: SteinerBooks 2010, as well as Andreas Neider: *Die Evolution von Gedächtnis und Erinnerung. Lesen in der Akasha-Forschung.* Stuttgart 2008, pp. 49-72.

9   Sergei O. Prokofieff: *Das Mysterium der Auferstehung im Lichte der Anthroposophie*. Stuttgart 2008, p. 57.
10 Rudolf Steiner: *Vorträge und Kurse über christlich-religiöses Wirken, II* [Lectures and courses on Christian religious work, vol. 2]. GA 343, p. 562.
11 Cf. Emil Bock: *The Three Years*. Edinburgh, Scotland: Floris Books 2006, ch.3.
12 Rudolf Steiner: *Die tieferen Geheimnisse des Menschheitswerdens im Lichte der Evangelien*. GA 117. Second edition, Dornach 1986, p. 64. In English: *Deeper Secrets in Human History. In the Light of the Gospel of St. Matthew*. Tr. D.S. Osmond; A.P. Shepherd. Great Barrington, MA: SteinerBooks 1985.
13 Ibid., p. 69.
14 Cf. Peter Selg: *Das Ereignis der Jordantaufe. Epiphanias im Urchristentum und in der Anthroposophie Rudolf Steiners*. Stuttgart 2008.
15 Rudolf Steiner: *The Fifth Gospel*. GA 148. Cf. also Peter Selg: *Rudolf Steiner and the Fifth Gospel; Insights into a New Understanding of the Christ Mystery*. Tr. Catherine E. Creeger. Great Barrington, MA: SteinerBooks 2010.
16 Ibid., p. 50ff, and Peter Selg: *Das Ereignis der Jordantaufe. Epiphanias im Urchristentum und in der Anthroposophie Rudolf Steiners*, p. 39ff.
17 Ibid., pp. 88ff.
18 Rudolf Steiner: *Das Geheimnis der Trinität*. GA 214. Second edition, Dornach 1980, p. 166. In English: *The Mystery of the Trinity and the Mission of the Spirit*. Hudson, NY: Anthroposophic Press 1991.
19 Rudolf Steiner: *Vorträge und Kurse über christlich-religiöses Wirken, II* [Lectures and courses on Christian religious work, vol. 2]. GA 343, p. 561f.
20 Rudolf Steiner: *Das Matthäus-Evangelium*. GA 123. Seventh edition, Dornach 1988, p. 191. In English: *According to Matthew*. Tr. Catherine E. Creeger. Great Barrington, MA: SteinerBooks 2003.
21 Rudolf Steiner: *Die geistige Führung des Menschen und*

der Menschheit. GA 15. Tenth edition, Dornach 1987, p. 76f. In English: *The Spiritual Guidance of the Individual and Humanity.* Tr. Samuel Desch. Great Barrington, MA: SteinerBooks 1991.

22   Peter Selg, op. cit., pp. 55ff.

23   Rudolf Steiner: *Ursprungsimpulse der Geisteswissenschaft* [Origin-impulses of spiritual science]. GA 96. Second edition, Dornach 1981, p. 24.

24   Rudolf Steiner: *Das christliche Mysterium.* GA 97. Second edition, Dornach 1981, p. 24. In English: *The Christian Mystery.* Tr. James H. Hindes. Great Barrington, MA: SteinerBooks 1998.

25   Rudolf Steiner: *Kosmogonie.* GA 94. Dornach 1979, p. 296. In English: *An Esoteric Cosmology.* Great Barrington, MA: SteinerBooks 2008.

26   Rudolf Steiner: *Ursprungsimpulse der Geisteswissenschaft* [Origin-impulses of spiritual science]. GA 96, p. 291f.

27   Rudolf Steiner: *Das Markus-Evangelium.* GA 139. Sixth edition, Dornach 1985, p. 130. In English: *The Gospel of St. Mark.* Tr. S. E. Easton. Great Barrington, MA: SteinerBooks 1966.

28   Rudolf Steiner: *Kosmogonie.* GA 94, p. 21. In English: *An Esoteric Cosmology.*

29   Rudolf Steiner: *Die okkulten Wahrheiten alter Mythen und Sagen* [The occult truths of ancient myths and sagas]. GA 92. Dornach 1999, p. 175.

30   Rudolf Steiner: *Die Theosophie des Rosenkreuzers.* GA 99. Seventh edition, Dornach 1985, p. 135. In English: *Rosicrucian Wisdom.* Forest Row, U.K.: Rudolf Steiner Press 2000.

31   Rudolf Steiner: *Menschengeschichte im Lichte der Geistesforschung* [Human history in the light of spiritual research]. GA 61. Second edition, Dornach 1983, p. 307f.

32   Rudolf Steiner: *Das christliche Mysterium.* GA 97, p. 149. In English: *The Christian Mystery.*

33   Rudolf Steiner: *Das Prinzip der spirituellen Ökonomie im Zusammenhang mit Wiederverkörperungsfragen.* GA 109. Third edition, Dornach 2000, p. 256. In English: *The*

Principle of Spiritual Economy. Tr. Peter Mollenhauer. Great Barrington, MA: SteinerBooks 1986.
34 Friedrich Rittelmeyer: *Briefe über das Johannes-Evangelium,* p. 226.
35 Rudolf Steiner: *Menschheitsentwicklung und Christus-Erkenntnis* [Human development and Christ knowledge]. GA 100. Third edition, Dornach 2006, p. 235.
36 Ibid., p. 213.
37 Rudolf Steiner: *Das Matthäus-Evangelium.* GA 123, p. 207. In English: *According to Matthew.*
38 Ibid., p. 213.
39 Ibid.
40 Cf. Rudolf Frieling: "Von den Gebets-Einsamkeiten des Christus Jesus." In: *Gesammelte Schriften zum Alten und Neuen Testament.* Vol. III, pp. 107-115.
41 Rudolf Frieling: "Die Verklärung auf dem Berge." In: *Gesammelte Schriften zum Alten und Neuen Testament.* Vol. IV. Stuttgart 1986, p. 201f.
42 Rudolf Steiner: *Vorträge und Kurse über christlich-religiöses Wirken,* II [Lectures and courses on Christian religious work, vol. 2]. GA 343, p. 297.
43 Ibid., p. 296.
44 Rudolf Steiner: *Das Markus-Evangelium.* GA 139, p. 175. In English: *The Gospel of St. Mark.*
45 Rudolf Steiner: *Das Matthäus-Evangelium.* GA 123, p. 196f. In English: *According to Matthew..*
46 Rudolf Steiner: *Aus der Akasha-Forschung. Das Fünfte Evan-gelium.* GA 148, p. 277. In English: *The Fifth Gospel.*
47 Ibid., p. 51f.
48 Ibid., p. 280.
49 Ibid., p. 150.
50 Ibid., p. 151.
51 Ibid., p. 321.
52 Ibid., p. 152.
53 Rudolf Steiner: *Das Johannes-Evangelium im Verhältnis zu den drei anderen Evangelien, besonders zu dem Lukas-Evangelium.* GA 112, p. 173. In English: *The Gospel of St.*

John and Its Relation to the Other Gospels. Tr. rev. Maria St. Goar. Great Barrington, MA: SteinerBooks 1982.
54 Rudolf Steiner: *Das Johannes-Evangelium im Verhältnis zu den drei anderen Evangelien, besonders zu dem Lukas-Evangelium*. GA 112, p. 173. In English: *The Gospel of St. John and Its Relation to the Other Gospels*.
55 Ibid., p. 279.
56 Ibid., p. 280.
57 Rudolf Steiner: *Der Tod als Lebenswandlung*. GA 182. Fourth edition, Dornach 1996, p. 167. In English: *Death as Metamorphosis of Life*. Tr. Sabine Seiler. Great Barrington, MA: SteinerBooks 2008.
58 Rudolf Steiner: *Die Verantwortung des Menschen für die Welt-Entwickelung* [The human being in relationship with the cosmos]. GA 203. Second edition, Dornach 1989, p. 232.
59 Rudolf Steiner. *Das Matthäus-Evangelium*. GA 123, p. 205f. In English: *According to Matthew*.
60 Ibid.
61 Ibid., p. 190.
62 Ibid., p. 191.
63 Rudolf Steiner: *Das Markus-Evangelium*. GA 139, p. 123. In English: *The Gospel of St. Mark*.
64 Rudolf Steiner: *Das Matthäus-Evangelium*. GA 123, p. 192. In English: *According to Matthew*.
65 Ibid.
66 Ibid., p. 193.
67 Ibid., p. 193.
68 Ibid., p. 205.
69 Ibid., p. 219.
70 Rudolf Steiner: *Das Markus-Evangelium*. GA 139, p. 120. In English: *The Gospel of St. Mark*.
71 Ibid.
72 Ibid.
73 Ibid., p. 121f.
74 Cf. Rudolf Steiner: *Zur Geschichte und aus den Inhalten der erkenntniskultischen Abteilung der Esoterischen Schule 1904 bis 1914*. GA 265. Dornach 1987, p. 431. In English:

Freemasonry and Ritual Work. Tr. John Wood. Great Barrington, MA: SteinerBooks 2007.
75 Rudolf Steiner: *Das Matthäus-Evangelium.* GA 123, p. 213f. In English: *According to Matthew.*
76 Ibid., p.215f.
77 Cf. Rudolf Steiner: *Die Evolution vom Gesichtspunkt des Wahrhaftigen.* GA 132. Seventh edition, Dornach 1999, p. 88ff In English: *Inner Experiences of Evolution.* Tr. Jann Gates. Great Barrington, MA: SteinerBooks 2009. *Vorstufen des Mysteriums von Golgatha.* GA 152, pp. 38ff./70f. In English: *Approaching the Mystery of Golgotha.* Tr. Michael Miller. Great Barrington, MA: SteinerBooks 2006. *Das Sonnenmysterium und das Mysterium von Tod und Auferstehung.* GA 211. Third edition, Dornach 2006, 131ff. In English: *The Sun Mystery.* Tr. Catherine E. Creeger. Great Barrington, MA: SteinerBooks 2006.
78 Rudolf Steiner: *Das Lukas-Evangelium.* GA 114. Ninth edition, Dornach 2001, p. 114. In English: *According to Luke.* Tr. Catherine E. Creeger. Great Barrington, MA: SteinerBooks 2001.
79 Cf Rudolf Frieling. "Die Verklärung auf dem Berge." In: *Gesammelte Schriften zum Alten und Neuen Testament.* Vol. IV, p. 232.
80 Ibid., p. 197.
81 Ibid., p. 203.
82 Ibid., p. 232.
83 Ibid., p. 200.
84 Ibid., p.254.
85 Ibid., p. 227.
86 Ibid., p. 330.
87 Rudolf Steiner: *Das christliche Mysterium.* GA 97, p. 20. In English: *The Christian Mystery.*
88 Ibid.
89 Rudolf Steiner: *Über die astrale Welt und das Devachan* [About the astral world and devachan]. GA 88. Dornach 1999, p. 232.
90 Rudolf Steiner: *Grundelemente der Esoterik* [Fundamentals of Esotericism]. GA 93a. Third edition, Dornach 1987, p. 63.

Notes   141

91 Rudolf Steiner: *Das Markus-Evangelium*. GA 139, p. 149. In English: *The Gospel of St. Mark*.
92 Rudolf Steiner: *Das Matthäus-Evangelium*. GA 123, p. 286. In English: *According to Matthew*.
93 Cf. Peter Selg: *Krankheit und Christus-Erkenntnis*. Second edition, Dornach 2003, pp. 19ff; and Peter Selg (ed.): *"Es war einer krank." Die Heilungen in den Evangelien*. Stuttgart 2003, pp. 15ff.
94 Rudolf Steiner: *Das Markus-Evangelium*. GA 139, p. 148. In English: *The Gospel of St. Mark*.
95 Rudolf Steiner: *Das Matthäus-Evangelium*. GA 123, p. 197f. In English: *According to Matthew*.
96 Rudolf Steiner: *Das Markus-Evangelium*. GA 139, p. 152. In English: *The Gospel of St. Mark*.
97 Rudolf Steiner: *Das Matthäus-Evangelium*. GA 123, p. 197f. In English: *According to Matthew*.
98 Rudolf Steiner: *Das Markus-Evangelium*. GA 139, p. 139. In English: *The Gospel of St. Mark*.
99 Rudolf Steiner: *Die okkulten Wahrheiten alter Mythen und Sagen* [The occult truths of ancient myths and sagas]. GA 92, p. 155.
100 Rudolf Steiner: *Das Markus-Evangelium*. GA 139, p. 156f. In English: *The Gospel of St. Mark*.
101 Rudolf Steiner: *Das christliche Mysterium*. GA 97, p. 20; cf. In English: *The Christian Mystery*. Also Rudolf Steiner: *Kosmogonie*. GA 94, pp. 216ff. *An Esoteric Cosmology*.
102 Rudolf Steiner: *Spirituelle Seelenlehre und Weltbetrachtung*. [Spiritual teachings about the soul and observation of the world]. GA 52. Second edition, Dornach 19856, p. 78f.
103 Rudolf Steiner: *Das Markus-Evangelium*. GA 139, p. 178. In English: *The Gospel of St. Mark*.
104 Rudolf Steiner: *Das Lukas-Evangelium*. GA 114, p. 205. In English: *According to Luke*.
105 Ibid.
106 Ibid., p. 206.
107 Rudolf Steiner: *Das Markus-Evangelium*. GA 139, p. 170. In English: *The Gospel of St. Mark*.

108 Rudolf Steiner: *Aus der Akasha-Forschung. Das Fünfte Evan-gelium.* GA 148, pp. 94ff. In English: *The Fifth Gospel.*
109 Ibid., p. 150ff.
110 Ibid., p. 279f.
111 Ibid., p. 321.
112 Ibid.
113 Rudolf Frieling: "Die drei Leidensverkündigungen." In: *Gesammelte Schriften zum Alten und Neuen Testament.* Vol. III, p. 98f.
114 Emil Bock: *The Three Years,* p. 221.
115 Friedrich Rittelmeyer: *Briefe über das Johannes-Evangelium,* p. 225.
116 Emil Bock: *The Three Years,* p. 222.
117 Rudolf Steiner: *Das Johannes-Evangelium im Verhältnis zu den drei anderen Evangelien, besonders zu dem Lukas-Evangelium.* GA 112, p. 253f. In English: *The Gospel of St. John and Its Relation to the Other Gospels.*
118 Cf. Friedrich Rittelmeyer: "Das Hohepriesterliche Gebet." In: *Briefe über das Johannes-Evangelium,* pp. 278-383.
119 Rudolf Frieling: "Von den Gebets-Einsamkeiten des Christus Jesus." In: *Gesammelte Schriften zum Alten und Neuen Testament.* Vol. III, p. 113.
120 Ibid., p. 114.
121 Rudolf Steiner: *Aus der Akasha-Forschung. Das Fünfte Evan-gelium.* GA 148, p. 151. In English: *The Fifth Gospel.*
122 Rudolf Steiner: *Das esoterische Christentum.* GA 130. Fourth edition, Dornach 1995, p. 222. In English: *Esoteric Christianity.* Tr. Matthew Barton. Forest Row, U.K.: Rudolf Steiner Press 2005.
123 Rudolf Frieling: "Von den Gebets-Einsamkeiten des Christus Jesus." In: *Gesammelte Schriften zum Alten und Neuen Testa-ment.* Vol. III, p. 115.
124 Rudolf Frieling. *Christentum und Islam. Der Geisteskampf um das Menschenbild.* Frankfurt 1981, p. 205.
125 Ibid.
126 Re: Judas cf. Ruth Ewertowski: *Judas. Verräter und Märtyrer.* Stuttgart 2000.

127 Rudolf Frieling: "Die Verleugnung des Petrus." In: *Gesammelte Schriften zum Alten und Neuen Testament*. Vol. III, p. 120.
128 Rudolf Steiner: *Das Markus-Evangelium*. GA 139, p. 170f. In English: *The Gospel of St. Mark*.
129 Rudolf Steiner: *Das esoterische Christentum*. GA 130, p. 283. In English: *Esoteric Christianity*.
130 Rudolf Steiner: *Von Jesus zu Christus*. GA 131. Seventh edition, Dornach 1988, p. 48. In English: *From Jesus to Christ*. Forest Row, U.K.: Rudolf Steiner Press 2005.
131 Rudolf Steiner: *Kosmogonie*. GA 94, p. 40. In English: *An Esoteric Cosmology*.
132 Ibid., p. 295.
133 Rudolf Steiner: *Ursprungsimpulse der Geisteswissenschaft* [Origin-impulses of spiritual science]. GA 96, p. 294.
134 Rudolf Steiner: *Das Johannes-Evangelium im Verhältnis zu den drei anderen Evangelien, besonders zu dem Lukas-Evangelium*. GA 112, p. 216. In English: *The Gospel of St. John and Its Relation to the Other Gospels*.
135 Rudolf Steiner: *Das Johannes-Evangelium*. GA 103. Eleventh edition, Dornach 1995, p. 209f. In English: *The Gospel of St. John*. Tr. Maud B. Monges. Great Barrington, MA: SteinerBooks 1984.
136 Rudolf Frieling: "Die sieben Worte am Kreuz." In: *Gesammelte Schriften zum Alten und Neuen Testament*. Vol. III, p. 127f.
137 Rudolf Steiner: *Das Johannes-Evangelium*. GA 103, p. 210. In English: *The Gospel of St. John*. Tr. Maud B. Monges. Great Barrington, MA: SteinerBooks 1984.
138 Rudolf Steiner: *Vorträge und Kurse über christlich-religiöses Wirken, V*. GA 346. Second edition, Dornach 2001, p. 128. In English: *The Book of Revelation*. Tr. Johanna Collis. Forest Row, U.K.: Rudolf Steiner Press 2008.
139 Rudolf Frieling: "Der Gang nach Emmaus." In: *Gesammelte Schriften zum Alten und Neuen Testament*. Vol. III, p. 150.
140 Rudolf Frieling: "Die sieben Oster-Geschichten in den Evangelien." In: *Gesammelte Schriften zum Alten und Neuen Testament*. Vol. III, p. 145.

141 Rudolf Frieling: *Der wunderbare Fischzug*. Ibid., p. 164.
142 Rudolf Steiner: *Das Matthäus-Evangelium*. GA 123, p. 252. In English: *According to Matthew*.
143 Rudolf Steiner: *Von Jesus zu Christus*. GA 131, p. 142. In English: *From Jesus to Christ*.
144 Rudolf Steiner: *Vom Leben des Menschen und der Erde* [On the life of the human being and of the earth]. GA 349, p. 250.
145 Rudolf Steiner: *Von Jesus zu Christus*. GA 131, p. 142. In English: *From Jesus to Christ*.
146 Rudolf Steiner: *Vom Leben des Menschen und der Erde* [On the life of the human being and of the earth]. GA 349, p. 250.
147 Emil Bock: "Bodily Resurrection." In: *The Three Years*, p. 248.
148 Rudolf Steiner: *Das esoterische Christentum*. GA 130, p. 122. In English: *Esoteric Christianity*.
149 Rudolf Steiner: *Das Markus-Evangelium*. GA 139, p. 133. In English: *The Gospel of St. Mark*.
150 Rudolf Steiner: *Vom Leben des Menschen und der Erde* [On the life of the human being and of the earth]. GA 349, p. 249.
151 Bock, op. cit., p. 250.
152 Rudolf Steiner: *Von Jesus zu Christus*. GA 131, p. 143. In English: *From Jesus to Christ*.
153 Rudolf Steiner: *Vom Leben des Menschen und der Erde* [On the life of the human being and of the earth]. GA 349, p. 249.
154 Rudolf Steiner: *Von Jesus zu Christus*. GA 131, p. 187. In English: *From Jesus to Christ*.
155 Emil Bock: *Die Drei Jahre*, p. 408. In English: *The Three Years*, Tr. Alfred Heidenreich 1995, p. 252.
156 Rudolf Steiner: *Das Sonnenmysterium und das Mysterium von Tod und Auferstehung*. GA 211, p. 130. In English: *The Sun Mystery*.
157 Rudolf Steiner: *Vorträge und Kurse über christlich-religiöses Wirken, V*. GA 346, p. 137. In English: *The Book of Revelation*.

158 Rudolf Steiner: *Das Sonnenmysterium und das Mysterium von Tod und Auferstehung*. GA 211, p. 137. In English: *The Sun Mystery*.
159 Cf. Emil Bock: "The Teaching of the Risen Christ. Gnostic Documents." In: *The Three Years*, pp. 252-258.
160 Emil Bock: *The Three Years*, p. 252.
161 Rudolf Steiner: *Das Geheimnis der Trinität*. GA 214, p. 166. In English: *The Mystery of the Trinity*.
162 Rudolf Steiner: *Das Sonnenmysterium und das Mysterium von Tod und Auferstehung*. GA 211, p. 104. In English: *The Sun Mystery*.
163 Ibid., p. 131f.
164 Ibid., p. 130.
165 Ibid., p. 108ff.
166 Rudolf Steiner: *Menschliches Selenleben und Geistesstreben im Zusammenhange mit Welt- und Erdenentwickelung* [Human soul life and spiritual striving in connection with world and earth development]. GA 212. Second edition, Dornach 1998, p. 107.
167 On the cosmic dimension of the resurrection and the resurrection-body, cf. Sergei O. Prokoffief: *Das Mysterium der Auferstehung*, pp. 82ff.
168 Rudolf Steiner: *Das Geheimnis der Trinität*. GA 214, p. 166f. In English: *The Mystery of the Trinity*.
169 Rudolf Steiner: *Menschenwesen, Menschenschicksal und Welt-Entwickelung* {Human being, human destiny, and world development]. GA 226. Fifth edition, Dornach 1988, p. 188.
170 Rudolf Steiner: *Esoterische Betrachtungen karmischer Zusammenhänge*. Vol. 2. GA 236. Sixth edition, Dornach 1988, pp. 249ff. In English: *Karmic Relationships 2*. Forest Row, U.K.: Rudolf Steiner Press 1997.
171 Rudolf Steiner: *Die geistige Vereinigung der Menschheit durch den Christus-Impuls*. GA 165. Third edition, Dornach 2006, p. 123. See in English: *The Universal Human*. Tr. Gilbert Church. Great Barrington, MA: SteinerBooks 2009.
172 Rudolf Steiner: *Aus der Akasha-Forschung. Das Fünfte Evan-gelium*. GA 148, p. 210. In English: *The Fifth Gospel*.

173 Rudolf Steiner: *Das Geheimnis der Trinität*. GA 214, p. 69. In English: *The Mystery of the Trinity*.
174 Rudolf Frieling: "Die Himmelfahrt des Christus." In: *Gesammelte Schriften zum Alten und Neuen Testament*. Vol. III, p. 175.
175 Ibid., p. 174.
176 Ibid.
177 Ibid.
178 Ibid.
179 Ibid., p. 175f.
180 Rudolf Steiner: *Die menschliche Seele in ihrem Zusammenhang mit göttlich-geistigen Individualitäten* [The human soul and its connection with divine-spiritual individualities]. GA 224, p. 148.
181 Ibid., p. 149.
182 Ibid., p. 149f.
183 Ibid., p. 150.
184 Ibid., p. 153.
185 Ibid., p. 151.
186 Rudolf Steiner: *Menschenwesen, Menschenschicksal und Welt-Entwickelung* {Human being, human destiny, and world development]. GA 226, p. 96.
187 Ibid., p. 129.
188 Rudolf Steiner: *Vom Leben des Menschen und der Erde* [On the life of the human being and of the earth]. GA 349, p. 251.
189 Emil Bock: *The Three Years*, p. 245.
190 Rudolf Steiner: *Die menschliche Seele in ihrem Zusammenhang mit göttlich-geistigen Individualitäten* [The human soul and its connection with divine-spiritual individualities]. GA 224, p. 153.
191 Rudolf Steiner: *Menschenwesen, Menschenschicksal und Welt-Entwickelung* {Human being, human destiny, and world development]. GA 226, p. 129.
192 Ibid., p. 96f.
193 Ibid., p. 96.
194 Rudolf Steiner: *Die Tempellegende und die Goldene Legende*.

GA 93. Third edition, Dornach 1991, p. 22. In English: *The Temple Legend*. Forest Row, U.K.: Rudolf Steiner Press 2002.
195 Rudolf Steiner: *Aus der Akasha-Forschung. Das Fünfte Evangelium*. GA 148, pp. 23ff. In English: *The Fifth Gospel*.
196 Ibid., pp.32ff.
197 Ibid., p. 25.
198 Cf. Emil Bock, "The Sphere of Enlightened Remembrance." In: *The Three Years*, Ch. XI, pp. 244-247.
199 Rudolf Steiner: *Aus der Akasha-Forschung. Das Fünfte Evangelium*. GA 148, p. 208. In English: *The Fifth Gospel*.
200 Ibid.
201 Ibid.
202 Ibid., p. 210.
203 Ibid.
204 Ibid., p. 209.
205 Ibid., p. 211.
206 Ibid., p. 208f.
207 Ibid., p. 210.
208 Ibid., p. 209.
209 Ibid., p. 213.
210 Rudolf Steiner: *Erfahrungen des Übersinnlichen. Die drei Wege der Seele zu Christus* [Experiences of the suprasensory. Three paths of the soul to Christ]. GA 143. Fourth edition, Dornach 1994, p. 182.
211 Rudolf Steiner: *Erdensterben und Weltenleben* [Earthly death and cosmic life]. GA 181. Third edition, Dornach 1981, p. 256.
212 Ibid., p. 260.
213 Rudolf Steiner: *Aus der Akasha-Forschung. Das Fünfte Evangelium*. GA 148, p. 40. In English: *The Fifth Gospel*.
214 Rudolf Steiner: *Das Geheimnis der Trinität*. GA 214, p. 69. In English: *The Mystery of the Trinity*.
215 Rudolf Steiner: *Die menschliche Seele in ihrem Zusammenhang mit göttlich-geistigen Individualitäten* [The human soul and its connection with divine-spiritual individualities]. GA 224, p.145.
216 Rudolf Steiner: *Aus der Akasha-Forschung. Das Fünfte Evangelium*. GA 148, p. 24. In English: *The Fifth Gospel*.

217 Rudolf Steiner: *Die menschliche Seele in ihrem Zusammenhang mit göttlich-geistigen Individualitäten* [The human soul and its connection with divine-spiritual individualities]. GA 224, p.154.
218 Rudolf Steiner: *Das Markus-Evangelium*. GA 139, p. 187. In English: *The Gospel of St. Mark*.
219 Rudolf Steiner: *Vorträge und Kurse über christlich-religiöses Wirken, II* [Lectures and courses on Christian religious work, vol. 2]. GA 343, p. 567.
220 Rudolf Steiner: *Die okkulten Wahrheiten alter Mythen und Sagen* [The occult truths of ancient myths and sagas]. GA 92, p. 152.
221 Rudolf Steiner: *Aus der Akasha-Forschung. Das Fünfte Evangelium*. GA 148, p. 22. In English: *The Fifth Gospel*.
222 Ibid., p. 20f.
223 Kurt von Wistinghausen: *Das neue Bekenntnis – Wege zum Credo*. Stuttgart 1963, p. 69.
224 Rudolf Steiner: *Mantrische Sprüche. Seelenübungen II*. [Soul-exercises: vol 2, Mantric verses 1903-1925]. GA 268. Dornach 199, p. 341. According to Marie Steiner-von Sivers, Rudolf Steiner described this prayer as the "esoteric Our Father or the Apostolic Our Father" (Ibid., p. 370).
225 Rudolf Steiner: *Ritualtexte für die Feiern des freien christlichen Religionsunterrichts*. [Ritual texts for the celebration of the free Christian religious instruction]. GA 269. Dornach 1997, pp. 85ff.

Ita Wegman Institute
for Basic Research into Anthroposophy

Pfeffinger Weg 1 A CH-4144 Arlesheim, Switzerland
www.wegmaninstitut.ch
e-mail: sekretariat@wegmaninstitut.ch

The Ita Wegman Institute for Basic Research into Anthroposophy is a non-profit research and teaching organization. It undertakes basic research into the lifework of Dr. Rudolf Steiner (1861–1925) and the application of Anthroposophy in specific areas of life, especially medicine, education, and curative education. Work carried out by the Institute is supported by a number of foundations and organizations and an international group of friends and supporters. The Director of the Institute is Prof. Dr. Peter Selg.